Harriet Beecher Stowe's

Uncle Tom's Cabin

Text by
Edward Tang
(M.A. New York University)
Department of American Studies
New York University
New York, New York

Illustrations by
Michael A. Kupka

 Research & Education Association

What **MAXnotes**® *Will Do for You*

This book is intended to help you absorb the essential contents and features of Harriet Beecher Stowe's *Uncle Tom's Cabin* and to help you gain a thorough understanding of the work. The book has been designed to do this more quickly and effectively than any other study guide.

For best results, this **MAXnotes** book should be used as a companion to the actual work, not instead of it. The interaction between the two will greatly benefit you.

To help you in your studies, this book presents the most up-to-date interpretations of every section of the actual work, followed by questions and fully explained answers that will enable you to analyze the material critically. The questions also will help you to test your understanding of the work and will prepare you for discussions and exams.

Meaningful illustrations are included to further enhance your understanding and enjoyment of the literary work. The illustrations are designed to place you into the mood and spirit of the work's settings.

The **MAXnotes** also include summaries, character lists, explanations of plot, and section-by-section analyses. A biography of the author and discussion of the work's historical context will help you put this literary piece into the proper perspective of what is taking place.

The use of this study guide will save you the hours of preparation time that would ordinarily be required to arrive at a complete grasp of this work of literature. You will be well prepared for classroom discussions, homework, and exams. The guidelines that are included for writing papers and reports on various topics will prepare you for any added work which may be assigned.

The **MAXnotes** will take your grades "to the max."

Dr. Max Fogiel
Program Director

Contents

> **Each Chapter includes List of Characters, Summary, Analysis, Study Questions and Answers, and Suggested Essay Topics.**

SECTION ONE

Introduction

The Life and Work of Harriet Beecher Stowe

Harriet Beecher Stowe was born on June 14, 1811, in Litchfield, Connecticut. She was raised in a family of ministers, two of them quite famous in their time: her father, Lyman Beecher, and her brother, Henry Ward Beecher. In fact, six of her seven brothers were ministers and she even married a clergyman, Calvin Stowe. Two of her sisters, Catharine and Isabella, became actively involved in reform movements, including education and women's rights.

Stowe herself became known as the celebrated author of *Uncle Tom's Cabin*. Written in 1852, nine years prior to the Civil War, the book stirred up much controversy among both Southerners and Northerners for its attack on slavery. Even then, the book quickly became a best seller, with one million copies sold within the first year of its publication. Afterwards, upon meeting Stowe at the White House in 1862, Abraham Lincoln supposedly quipped: "So this is the little lady who wrote the book that made this great war."

Prior to this renown, Stowe aided her sister Catharine at the Hartford Female Seminary from 1824 to 1832. The family moved to Cincinnati, Ohio in 1832 when Lyman Beecher became the director of the Lane Theological Seminary. Here, Stowe came into contact with such abolitionists, or anti-slavery people, as Theodore Weld and Salmon Chase. She also met her husband Calvin, who was a professor of religion at the school. They married in 1836.

Stowe developed an early interest in writing and began to publish her work in 1833. Ten years later, a collection of her short stories entitled *The Mayflower* appeared. The task of writing, however, was never easy for her. She constantly had to find a balance be-tween her life as an author and as a wife and a mother to seven children. As she put it: "I mean to have money enough to have my house kept in the best manner and yet to have time for reflection and that preparation for the education of my children which every mother needs."

The Stowes moved and traveled a great deal. In 1850, they re-turned from the Midwest to New England, where Calvin taught at Bowdoin College in Maine. The family relocated to Andover, Mas-sachusetts in 1852, and then to Hartford, Connecticut in 1864. They also maintained a summer residence in Florida from 1868 to 1884. At three intervals during the 1850s, Stowe journeyed to Europe.

Much of these experiences contributed to Stowe's prolific writ-ing. She published four novels about the New England region: *The Minister's Wooing* (1859), *The Pearl of Orr's Island* (1862), *Oldtown Folks* (1869), and *Poganuc People* (1878). *Sunny Memories of For-eign Lands* (1854) was gleaned from her European travels, and *Palmetto-Leaves* (1873) from her insights on Florida. Stowe also wrote for several magazines, such as the *Atlantic Monthly*, as well as other volumes of essays, novels, and histories. None of these projects, however, received the widespread notice that made *Uncle Tom's Cabin* one of the most popular novels in the nineteenth cen-tury. Harriet Beecher Stowe died on July 1, 1896.

Historical Background

Harriet Beecher Stowe composed *Uncle Tom's Cabin* during the tumultuous pre-Civil War period. She developed an intense aboli-tionist attitude, combining it with her Christian faith, as a result of living in Ohio. Because of its proximity to Kentucky, a slave state, Cincinnati served as a way-station for slaves escaping north to Canada. Stowe based several characters and incidents in *Uncle Tom's Cabin* on her own family's and friends' experiences helping runaway slaves.

Uncle Tom's Cabin was Stowe's response to the politics of her time. As part of the Compromise of 1850, Northern and Southern congressmen passed the Fugitive Slave Law. This legislation or-dered that Southern slave catchers could retain the aid of any law enforcers in the North to search for fugitive slaves. By this logic, the North and the South became direct partners in the perpetuation of slavery.

Stowe wanted to indict the system of slavery itself, and not solely individuals. She argued that Christianity provided the moral force to overcome the evils of her day, both for slaves and masters, as well as for indifferent Northerners. The character, Uncle Tom, personifies her ideal of Christian humility and goodness.

Uncle Tom's Cabin has been translated into numerous foreign languages, and has sold in the millions. Plays, songs, poetry, films, and other novels have been based on the book.

Modern critics have displayed various reactions to *Uncle Tom's Cabin*. Until recently, most scholars have ignored Stowe's work, or have decried its outdated, sentimental tone. Such African American writers as James Baldwin and Richard Wright have denounced Stowe's racist portrayal of slaves. Others have felt uncomfortable with the author's views supporting women's limited roles in society. More critics, however, are beginning to pay close attention to the novel in light of its historical context. Whatever the response, *Uncle Tom's Cabin* will continue to elicit diverse interpretations for some time to come.

Master List of Characters

Mr. and Mrs. Shelby—*kind owners of Uncle Tom in Kentucky.*

Young Master George—*the Shelbys' son.*

Haley—*slave trader who buys Uncle Tom from the Shelbys, and then sells him further South.*

Eliza—*servant to Mrs. Shelby, mother of Harry and is married to George Harris.*

Harry—*son of Eliza and George Harris.*

George Harris—*husband of Eliza, father of Harry, works in Mr. Wilson's factory.*

Uncle Tom—*Christian slave of Shelbys', married to Aunt Chloe.*

Aunt Chloe—*Uncle Tom's wife, cook on Shelby plantation.*

Mose and Pete—*children of Tom and Chloe.*

Sam and Andy—*slaves on the Shelby plantation.*

Mr. Symmes—*helps Eliza and Harry onshore after they run across ice floes on the Ohio River to escape from Haley.*

Tom Loker—*acquaintance of Haley's, slave catcher who looks for Eliza and Harry.*

Marks—*Tom Loker's conniving companion.*

Senator John Bird—*Congressman who supports the Fugitive Slave Law, but ultimately helps Eliza and Harry escape.*

Mrs. Mary Bird—*Senator Bird's Christian wife, who argues against her husband's politics and convinces him to aid fugitives.*

John Van Trompe—*a neighbor of the Birds.*

Mr. Wilson—*George Harris's considerate employer at a factory.*

a drover—*a cattle driver who talks with Mr. Wilson about slavery.*

Mr. Harris—*George Harris's harsh master.*

Lucy—*woman whom Haley buys and separates from her child; she drowns herself in despair.*

Aunt Hagar and Albert—*mother and son whom Haley separates by buying the son.*

Simeon and Rachel Halliday—*Quaker couple who assist Eliza and Harry, reunites them with George Harris when he runs from a harsh master.*

Ruth Stedman—*a Quaker friend and neighbor of the Hallidays.*

Augustine St. Clare—*little Eva's father and Marie St. Clare's husband, Uncle Tom's second benevolent owner after buying him from Haley, lives in New Orleans.*

Eva—*saintly daughter of St. Clares', befriends Uncle Tom.*

Mammy—*St. Clares' family servant.*

Marie St. Clare—*Augustine St. Clare's pouting and selfish wife, Little Eva's mother.*

Miss Ophelia—*Augustine's efficient Vermont cousin who comes to visit.*

Phineas Fletcher—*Quaker who helps the Harris family escape, fends off Tom Loker.*

Jim and his mother—*two slaves who runaway with the Harris family.*

Old Dinah—*cook in St. Clares' home.*

Prue—*slave woman from another house who visits St. Clares' and is often drunk, whipped to death by a hard master.*

Alfred St. Clare—*Augustine's twin brother who manages a plantation in Louisiana.*

Henrique—*Alfred's son, Little Eva's cousin.*

Dodo—*Henrique's boy servant.*

Topsy—*eight- or nine-year-old slave girl whom Augustine buys for Miss Ophelia to educate.*

Rosa, Jane, and Adolph—*Augustine's haughty servants.*

Mr. Skeggs—*keeper of a slave warehouse in which St. Clares' servants are held before being sold on auction block.*

Sambo—*a slave in Mr. Skeggs's warehouse.*

Emmeline—*religious fifteen-year-old girl sold with Uncle Tom to Simon Legree.*

Susan—*Emmeline's mother.*

Simon Legree—*severe and tough-fisted master of a rundown plantation on the Red River in Louisiana, buys Emmeline and Uncle Tom.*

Sambo and Quimbo—*Simon Legree's brutal slave drivers, slaves themselves.*

Lucy—*slave whom Simon Legree buys for Sambo; Uncle Tom helps her in the cotton fields.*

Cassy—*Simon Legree's fiery slave mistress who escapes with Emmeline, discovered to be Eliza Harris's long-lost mother.*

Aunt Dorcas—*Quaker woman who nurses Tom Loker back to health.*

Mrs. Smyth—*Quaker woman from Canada who helps the Harris family escape through disguises.*

Madame de Thoux (Emily)—*woman whom Master George meets after burying Uncle Tom and traveling north, discovered to be George Harris's long-lost sister.*

Little Eliza—*Eliza and George Harris's daughter, Cassy's granddaughter, who is born free in Canada.*

Summary of the Novel

Several stories intertwine throughout *Uncle Tom's Cabin*, but they all center on two main plots. One plot focuses on the Harris family, the other on Uncle Tom.

Mr. Shelby is a considerate master, but he must sell Tom to Haley, the slave trader, to pay off some debts. Eliza, Mrs. Shelby's servant, rightly fears that her son Harry will also be sold to Haley. She escapes to Ohio, taking Harry with her. Along the way, Eliza is assisted by Senator and Mrs. Bird, as well as a Quaker community. George Harris, Eliza's husband, runs away too after learning that his master refuses to lend him any longer to Mr. Wilson, a generous factory owner. The Harris family eventually reaches the safety of Canada, after being pursued unsuccessfully by slave catchers.

Meanwhile, St. Clare purchases Tom from Haley after Little Eva befriends the pious slave. Miss Ophelia, St. Clare's cousin from New England, visits and manages the St. Clare household in New Orleans. She also takes in Topsy as her ward. Eva dies after a prolonged illness, and a mournful St. Clare decides to free Tom. St. Clare is murdered, however, before he can draw up the papers. Tom is sold to Simon Legree, who runs a plantation in Louisiana. Legree beats Tom to death when the slave refuses to confess the whereabouts of Cassy and Emmeline, two of Legree's slaves who have run away. Cassy joins the Harrises in Canada, and they relocate to Africa.

Estimated Reading Time

Uncle Tom's Cabin is 451 pages long, and should take approximately 15-18 hours to read. The book consists of 45 chapters, and reading breaks can be taken after every two or three chapters.

Uncle Tom's Cabin

Chapter 1

New Characters:

Mr. Shelby: *benevolent owner of a Kentucky plantation*

Mrs. Shelby: *Mr. Shelby's religious wife*

Haley: *a slave trader*

Eliza: *Mrs. Shelby's servant, Harry's mother*

Harry: *four- or five-year-old son of Eliza*

Summary

The book opens with a scene in which Mr. Shelby and Haley the slave trader are discussing business matters on Shelby's plantation in Kentucky. Mr. Shelby, a gentleman planter described as "a fair average kind of man, good-natured and kindly," has fallen into debt and must sell Uncle Tom, a trustworthy servant. Mr. Shelby vouches for Tom's good working habits and Christian character. Haley, however, desires that more slaves be added to the deal to cover the debt. Little Harry, a boy slave, playfully interrupts the meeting and entertains the men with singing and dancing. Eliza, Harry's mother and Mrs. Shelby's personal servant, comes to retrieve her son. After they leave, Haley tries to convince Mr. Shelby to sell Eliza and Harry. Mr. Shelby refuses to sell Eliza out of respect for his wife, but he reluctantly considers parting with Harry.

Eliza overhears some of the two men's conversation when she takes away Harry and proceeds to tell Mrs. Shelby her worries. Mrs. Shelby is unaware of her husband's troubled financial status, and naively reassures Eliza that nothing will happen to her or her child. Mrs. Shelby is portrayed as "a woman of high class, both intellectually and morally."

Analysis

The reader is introduced to the conscience-stricken Mr. Shelby, who has fallen on hard times, and the greedy slave trader, Haley. Despite being a refined gentleman and humane slave owner, Mr. Shelby becomes caught in the morally distressing situation of dealing in human property. He treats his slaves kindly, almost as if they are a larger part of the family. Because the slaves are considered as humans and as property, their status only makes Mr. Shelby's decision to sell some of them more painful. Mr. Shelby chooses to sell Uncle Tom to cover some debts he owes to Haley. Tom at this point does not appear in the chapter, but the reader learns about him from Mr. Shelby's description. He emphasizes that Tom had been converted to Christianity four years ago, and can be trusted with various chores around the plantation. Since Tom is a valuable servant, Mr. Shelby hopes that the sale will be enough to end his debt.

Haley, on the other hand, is the opposite in character to Mr. Shelby. The slave trader is portrayed as "a short, thick-set man, with coarse, commonplace features,…a low man who is trying to elbow his way upward in the world." Being shrewd and greedy, Haley is aware of Mr. Shelby's financial situation and takes advantage of it, asking for another slave in addition to Tom to settle the debt. When little Harry and Eliza enter the room, Haley offers to take them both. Mr. Shelby initially balks at Haley's bartering methods. As he states to the slave trader: "I'm a humane man, and I hate to take the boy from his mother, sir." Mr. Shelby's humanity is flawed, however, by his own financial mismanagement. He eventually must carry out what he hates to do: take Harry away from Eliza.

A major theme emerges in this chapter and reappears throughout the book: the emotional strain slavery places on families, both black and white. The author emphasizes that the break up of slave families is inhuman. As will be seen later, slavery's evils also affect slave owners and traders. Haley is dehumanized by his business. He views slaves as property and thinks nothing of separating a mother and her children. Mr. Shelby, although a kind man, must still barter with Haley, thus becoming dehumanized as well. Mrs. Shelby's religious principles will be tested later when she confronts the reality of slavery.

The horrors of slavery are more immediately understood through the experiences of the slaves themselves. At several times further in the novel, Harriet Beecher Stowe addresses the reader directly by asking how anyone would feel if their children were forcibly taken from them.

The author uses a variety of stylistic devices. She employs foreshadowing by setting the scene during a late afternoon "of a chilly February day." This description heightens Mr. Shelby's depressed mood, and also hints at the bleak future for Uncle Tom, Eliza, and Harry.

Stowe depicts her characters through their dialect. Haley speaks in a rough, backwoods language. Regarding slaves, he unfeelingly says: "Lor bless ye, yes! These critters an't like white folks, you know; they gets over things, only manage right." Haley's manner of talking reflects the coarseness of his occupation and his whole character.

Study Questions

1. Why does Mr. Shelby need to sell some of his slaves?

2. Describe why Mr. Shelby thinks that Uncle Tom is a responsible servant.

3. What story does Haley tell to Mr. Shelby in regard to selling slaves?

4. What does Harry do to unintentionally attract Haley's notice?

5. How does Haley view Mr. Shelby's kindness toward slaves?

6. What is Mr. Shelby's religious position compared with Mrs. Shelby's?

7. What does Eliza suspect about Mr. Shelby's meeting with Haley?

8. How does Mrs. Shelby detect that something is wrong with Eliza?

9. Why does Mrs. Shelby not believe in Eliza's fears that Mr. Shelby will sell Harry?

10. Despite benevolent masters such as Mr. Shelby, what does the author point to regarding the inevitable failure of treating slaves like family?

Answers

1. Mr. Shelby must sell some slaves, because he is in debt to Haley.

2. Mr. Shelby trusts Tom with responsibilities because Tom is honest and pious. Mr. Shelby had even sent Tom to Cincinnati on a business matter and Tom returned afterwards instead of fleeing.

3. Haley tells Mr. Shelby of an incident in which a trader bought a woman, but did not want her child. Separated roughly from her baby, the slave woman died from overwhelming grief. Haley reassuringly says that he would have treated the situation more gently and diplomatically.

4. Harry playfully interrupts the meeting between Haley and Mr. Shelby, singing and dancing at Mr. Shelby's request. Haley immediately thinks that Harry could be sold at great profit as a waiter.

5. Haley views Mr. Shelby's kindness toward the slaves as wrongheaded since it gives them unrealistic expectations of a stable family life.

6. Unlike his wife, Mr. Shelby is not particularly religious. He does, however, revere Mrs. Shelby's opinions and believes that she "had piety and benevolence enough for two."

7. Eliza suspects that Mr. Shelby will sell her son Harry to Haley.

8. Mrs. Shelby detects that something is on Eliza's mind when Eliza works distractedly and accidentally breaks a washpitcher and upsets a table.

9. Mrs. Shelby thinks that Eliza's fears are imagined, because she cannot believe that Mr. Shelby would sell any of his slaves, much less deal with slave traders. Mrs. Shelby believes that the servants are part of the family.

10. The author stresses that the law considers slaves as things rather than as humans. They can then be bought or sold regardless of personal attachments.

Suggested Essay Topics

1. Describe Mr. Shelby's relationship to and views on his slaves. What difficulties arise from his position?

2. Describe Haley's opinions on the slave trading business. In what ways is he being harsh, or is he being realistic?

Chapters 2 and 3

New Characters:

George Harris: *Eliza's husband and Harry's father*

Mr. Harris: *George's hard plantation master*

A kind manufacturer: *George's employer at a factory, as yet unnamed*

Summary

The two chapters here include the personal histories of George and Eliza Harris. The reader learns that Eliza had been raised from childhood by Mrs. Shelby. Eliza then met and married George, a slave on a nearby plantation. Hired out by his master, Mr. Harris, George works at a factory, in which he invents a hemp-cleaning machine. Because of George's diligence and handiness, he becomes a favorite among his employer and fellow laborers. During this period of their lives, George is allowed great freedom in his work, and Eliza has given birth to Harry.

Mr. Harris, however, is envious of his slave's success and popularity. George is taken back to the plantation, where he is "put to

the meanest drudgery of the farm." In the meantime, George keeps his anger from showing. George's former employer visits the plantation, and tries to persuade Mr. Harris to let George return to work at the factory, but to no avail.

When George visits Eliza at the Shelby plantation, he recounts the hardships of laboring on his master's farm and the unfair treatment he receives. Beaten and tired, he exclaims: "I wish I were dead!" His attitude frightens Eliza, and she tells him to trust in God. George, however, confesses that his troubles appear too overwhelming; he cannot find comfort in religion. He resolves to escape to Canada, and then buy Eliza's and Harry's freedom. He concludes that despite the risks involved, he would rather die than be captured and returned to his present state of servility.

Analysis

Several incidents occur that threaten the Harris family, all because of its slave status. Earlier, in Chapter 1, Eliza worries that her son will be taken from her and sold. Chapters 2 and 3 depict the whims of George's tyrannical master, Mr. Harris (slaves took the surname of their masters). Although George works well in the factory, his owner is resentful of his accomplishments. By taking George away from the factory, Mr. Harris asserts his authority on his own property, despite others' protests.

The theme of maintaining a family in the face of slavery also concerns Mrs. Shelby, who has a long developed fondness for Eliza, having raised her almost like a daughter. Mrs. Shelby had even encouraged the marriage between Eliza and George, and had taken an active part in the festivities. She displays a maternal concern for them. Eliza and George in turn feel that their relationship is sanctified by the marriage ceremony, and their son Harry makes the family whole.

The benevolent factory owner is never identified by name in this chapter, but will be subsequently in the novel. The author uses a dialogue between the manufacturer and Mr. Harris to reveal the nature of slavery. The kindly employer thinks that George is well-adapted to the business and treats him humanely. To this, the hard master replies: "It's a free country, sir; the man's mine, and I do what I please with him,—that's it!" This statement is ironic.

Although a slave, George is recognized by his master as a man, not a thing. Mr. Harris, as a man with rights, is at liberty to do whatever he wants, including the freedom to deny George the same rights.

The irony is further developed when George discusses his miserable situation with Eliza. Regarding his owner, George declares, "what right has he to me? I'm a man as much as he is." The terrors of slavery are emphasized when George wishes that he had never been born. As a human person regarded as property, he feels that life is not worth living. The repetition of this statement will be made by other slaves in later chapters.

Eliza tries to calm her husband by asking him to have faith. She advocates the Christian principles of patience and humility, taught to her by Mrs. Shelby. Like Mr. Shelby, however, George is a decent person, but not a religious one. He cannot see the justice of his circumstances, and proclaims that he would rather die than be a slave any longer.

Study Questions

1. Why does George's master take him away from the factory?

2. What makes George hold his temper?

3. What earlier tragedy did Eliza go through in her marriage?

4. What does the good-hearted factory employer offer to persuade Mr. Harris to let George stay?

5. What does Mr. Harris think about George's hemp-cleaning machine?

6. Describe what George tells to Eliza about his experiences on the Harris plantation.

7. Describe what Mr. Harris has planned for George.

8. Why does Eliza fail at first to understand George's situation?

9. How does George explain to Eliza the reality of their marriage?

10. What does George request that Eliza do for him before he leaves?

Answers

1. After seeing George display his talent and good manners, Mr. Harris felt inferior and became determined to put George back in his place.

2. George holds his temper when the sympathetic employer at the factory promises to help him later.

3. Two of Eliza's children died before she gave birth to Harry.

4. The factory owner offers Mr. Harris more financial compensation.

5. Mr. Harris believes that George invented the hemp-cleaning machine to save time and labor for only himself.

6. George tells Eliza that he was whipped for trying to stop Mr. Harris's son from beating a horse. He also explains that Mr. Harris forces him to kill his own dog because it was eating too much at Mr. Harris's expense.

7. Mr. Harris wants George to settle down with a woman on the plantation and ignore Eliza. Otherwise, Mr. Harris would sell George further south to harsher work conditions.

8. Eliza fails to understand the extremity of her husband's circumstances because she herself had been treated well on the Shelby plantation. Her religious beliefs center on patience and faith when troubled times come.

9. George explains to his wife that their marriage is really nonexistent in the eyes of the law. As slaves, they cannot be married, which is why George wishes that he had never been born. To have known happiness and then have it taken away is a worse feeling.

10. George asks Eliza to pray for him because he believes in her faith.

Suggested Essay Topics

1. Compare and contrast George's character to his master's. What does Mr. Harris's actions lead George to conclude about slavery?

2.   Compare George's sense of religion to Eliza's. Why is he unsure of his own faith, but confident in Eliza's?

Chapters 4 and 5

New Characters:

Uncle Tom: *Shelby's devout and trusted slave*

Aunt Chloe: *Tom's wife, a cook for the Shelbys*

Master George: *thirteen-year-old son of Mr. and Mrs. Shelby*

Mose, Pete, and the baby: *Tom's and Chloe's children*

Summary

Chapter 4 opens with a description of Uncle Tom's cabin, "a small log building" near the plantation house. Inside, Aunt Chloe prepares dinner, fixing a variety of dishes. She is the head cook on the Shelby plantation, and her talents are known throughout the neighborhood. Also in the cabin are the three children of Uncle Tom and Aunt Chloe. Here the reader is introduced to Uncle Tom, the main character. He is described as "Mr. Shelby's best hand." Tom's character is "self-respecting and dignified, yet united with a confiding and humble simplicity."

At this time, young Master George, the Shelbys' son, is teaching Tom to write. George stays for dinner and talks to Aunt Chloe about neighborhood gossip. Mose and Pete, the two older children, play with the baby. After dinner, Tom's cabin is the meeting place in which the plantation's slaves gather to worship. They sing hymns, and Master George remains to read some Bible passages. Uncle Tom speaks to and prays for the group. He is looked upon as "a sort of patriarch in religious matters."

The scene lastly shifts to the Shelby house. Mr. Shelby and Haley engage in last minute business, signing the bills of sale for Uncle Tom and Eliza's son, Harry. Mr. Shelby then reminds Haley to try to find a good owner for Tom.

Chapter 5 begins where the previous chapter had left off. After Haley leaves, Mrs. Shelby asks her husband about his visitor. She

explains that Eliza had been upset earlier, having overheard Haley's offer for Harry. Mr. Shelby hesitantly admits that Haley is a slave trader, and that Uncle Tom and Harry were sold to him.

Mrs. Shelby is astounded by this news. She tells Mr. Shelby that she feels a certain responsibility toward the servants. As she states: "I have cared for them, instructed them, watched over them, and known all their little cares and joys, for years." Mrs. Shelby also had taught them the benefits of Christianity. She thinks that money should not separate families, and exclaims, "This is God's curse on slavery!" Mrs. Shelby even offers to contribute whatever is needed to keep Tom and Harry. Mr. Shelby, however, informs his wife that the deal with Haley has already been made.

Eliza overhears the Shelbys' discussion and immediately decides to run away with Harry. After hurriedly packing their clothes, Eliza stops by Uncle Tom's cabin late that night. Tom and Chloe are still awake since their prayer meeting had just finished. Eliza tells them about Mr. Shelby's trade with Haley. Horrified, Chloe advises Tom to flee with Eliza and Harry. Tom declines, saying that he cannot break his master's trust. The chapter closes with Eliza and Harry heading toward Ohio and hopefully on to Canada.

Analysis

In Chapter 4, the reader obtains several impressions about Uncle Tom and his family. Tom is kind, self-respecting, and intensely religious. Aunt Chloe cooks and cares for the Shelbys as well as her own family. Master George relates easily with his father's servants. He teaches Tom how to write, chats with them, and participates in their prayer meeting. Tom's and Chloe's children run around playfully. The cabin serves as the family living quarters and as a meeting house for other slaves. Everyone is familiar and friendly with one another. Within this slave community, the reader learns about the daily rituals that hold together the family. People eat, learn, and worship under one roof. These scenes suggest the characters' close-knit relationships with one another, forming an extended sense of family.

The scene then switches to Mr. Shelby and Haley. Mr. Shelby's conscience weighs on him because of the "disagreeable business" with Haley. The reader senses that Shelby's debt is great since he must sell Tom, his "best hand." The reason for the trade, however, is not due to anyone's fault or responsibility. It is rather the "circumstances," as Mr. Shelby points out. He defensively reasons that his debts force him to do what he otherwise would not usually consider. Haley responds similarly; he must earn a living, and tries to avoid the sole blame for slavery's evils. The trader's rationale is further developed in later chapters.

These circumstances, however, have larger consequences. Uncle Tom will be separated from his family; Eliza's child will be sold from her; the Shelbys argue over the meaning of owning slaves. By confronting her husband, Mrs. Shelby realizes the extent of slavery's injustice. Previously, she had assumed that Mr. Shelby would never sell his most trusted servant, Tom. Mrs. Shelby also had refused to believe that little Harry would be included in the trade. She even had assured Eliza about the impossibility of this scenario under the assumption that her husband would not separate families for monetary gain.

The conversation between Mr. and Mrs. Shelby is tense. Mr. Shelby explains that Tom and Harry would bring the highest prices to settle his debt. Alarmed by his wife's reaction and views on slavery, he jokingly calls her an abolitionist, or anti-slavery supporter. Mrs. Shelby, on the other hand, cannot cope with the hypocrisy of their situation. She had taught the servants familial duties and her religious faith. Now Tom's and Eliza's families will be torn apart for financial reasons. Monetary concerns appear more important than the sanctity of family, contradicting Mrs. Shelby's teachings.

The author relies on ambivalence to portray the Shelbys. For Mrs. Shelby, the situation is complex. On the one hand, she is married to Mr. Shelby, a slave holder. Eliza is her personal servant whom the Shelbys own. These relationships are based on the idea that slaves are property. On the other hand, Mrs. Shelby treats them as family members and has motherly attachments to them. The question of whether slaves are property or human beings leads her to curse slavery. She declares: "It is a sin to hold a slave under laws like ours." To Mrs. Shelby, slaves cannot be "human property," a paradox. Mrs. Shelby ultimately rejects the idea that slaves are both humans and property. She resolves her ambivalence by choosing to condemn slavery on moral grounds and viewing slaves as humans with souls.

Mr. Shelby is also ambivalent, but he reaches the opposite conclusion to that of his wife's. He knows that Uncle Tom is his best servant. The task of separating Harry from Eliza is too horrible for him to imagine. However, Mr. Shelby is in financial trouble. If he fails to sell some of his slaves, he will lose his whole plantation. Mr. Shelby thus decides to sacrifice Tom and Harry.

The author uses other stylistic devices in these chapters. Both Tom and Chloe speak in dialect, as do other slaves in the book. Tom says about his baby: "Aint she a peart young un?"

The chapters include the theme of loyalty vs. betrayal. Aunt Chloe believes that the only way to protest Mr. Shelby's decision is for Tom to escape. Tom, however, refuses to betray Mr. Shelby. Although Tom and the other slaves had believed that they would remain together as a family, Mr. Shelby betrays their trust. Tom's faith and honesty prove stronger than his master's. Thoughts of her family also influence Eliza's decisions and loyalties. As a mother, Eliza realizes that she must leave with Harry to protect what remains of her family. She determines that the risks are worth taking. By running to Canada and seeking her husband, Eliza will try to keep her family intact.

Study Questions

1. What hangs over the fireplace in Uncle Tom's cabin?
2. What three things does young Master George do on his visit to the cabin?
3. How does Master George jest with Aunt Chloe?
4. From which part of the Bible does Master George read?
5. What makes Mrs. Shelby question her husband about Haley?
6. What does Mrs. Shelby call herself to justify her arguments against selling Harry and Tom?
7. Why does Mrs. Shelby call the deal to sell Harry and Tom "God's curse on slavery"?
8. How does Mr. Shelby defend himself on religious grounds?
9. Why does Tom decide to stay when Eliza tells him of Mr. Shelby's intentions?
10. What last instructions does Eliza leave for Tom and Chloe?

Answers

1. A portrait of George Washington hangs over the fireplace.

2. Master George teaches Tom how to write, he stays for dinner, and he reads at the prayer meeting.

3. Master George jests with Aunt Chloe by telling her that a servant on another plantation is supposed to be a better cook than her. Chloe pretends to take great offense at this suggestion.

4. George reads the last chapters from Revelations.

5. Mrs. Shelby questions her husband because of Eliza's earlier fears of Haley's offer for Harry.

6. Mrs. Shelby calls herself a "Christian woman."

7. Mrs. Shelby thinks that both masters and slaves are cursed by slavery. Masters sin for dealing in humans as property. Slaves suffer because they cannot live as human beings.

8. Mr. Shelby points to some ministers who defend slavery.

9. Aside from his trustworthiness, Tom remains because he thinks that it is better for him to be sold than to have the whole plantation ruined.

10. She tells them to let her husband George know what has happened, if they see him.

Suggested Essay Topics

1. How do Uncle Tom and Aunt Chloe raise their children? Are they strict or lenient? In what ways?

2. Describe Eliza's thoughts and emotions as she learns about and decides her fate. What does she remember about her life growing up on the plantation? What are her fears about the future?

3. Why does Mrs. Shelby feel that both masters and slaves are cursed by slavery? How do the Shelbys suffer? How do the servants on the plantation suffer?

Chapter 6

New Characters:

Sam and Andy: *slaves on the Shelby plantation*

Summary

Mr. and Mrs. Shelby are brought news the following morning of Eliza's escape. Mrs. Shelby reacts gratefully while her husband is less than thankful. The surprising report spreads throughout the house as the servants tell one another about the event.

Haley arrives at the plantation to pick up Uncle Tom and Harry. Much to his annoyance, he too learns of Eliza's and Harry's escape. He tells Mr. Shelby about the unfairness of the situation. Mr. Shelby responds angrily that he will not be accused of helping the fugitives run away. He then invites Haley in for breakfast to discuss what can be done.

Sam and Andy, two slaves on the Shelby plantation, are introduced in this chapter. They prepare some horses to aid Haley in his pursuit of Eliza. Andy, however, explains to Sam that Mrs. Shelby does not want Eliza caught. In fact, Mrs. Shelby tells Sam not to ride too fast because the horses should not be exhausted. Sam understands her implications to delay the chase.

To stir up trouble for Haley, Sam places a beechnut under the trader's saddle. When Haley mounts his horse, the animal bolts and throws its rider. Shouting and waving, Sam pretends to chase Haley's horse. He then explains to Haley that the horse must be rubbed down and rested after its exertions. Mrs. Shelby meanwhile invites Haley to stay for dinner, further detaining the hunt for Eliza and Harry.

Analysis

Tensions arise between Mr. Shelby and Haley when both discover Eliza's disappearance. The two immediately realize that Eliza has fled to keep Harry from being taken from her. Despite having a bill of sale for Harry, Haley winds up with only Tom. He indirectly blames Mr. Shelby for failing to keep his part of the bargain. As Haley complains, "I did expect fair dealing in this matter, I con-

fess." Mr. Shelby is insulted by Haley's insinuations that he would cheat the trader.

The author relies on humor in her depiction of Sam and Andy. Both speak in dialect, and assume to know more than they sometimes do. When Mr. Shelby orders them to saddle horses to accompany Haley, Sam and Andy delay their preparations. Both are aware of how Mrs. Shelby feels about Eliza. They attempt to provide Eliza with enough time and distance to escape successfully. Sam and Andy are loyal to both Mrs. Shelby and Eliza, even at the risk of appearing to disobey Mr. Shelby.

Sam at first is confused about the situation. He thinks that because Mrs. Shelby loves Eliza, she would want her servant returned. Andy explains that this is not the case. Andy's opinion is verified by Mrs. Shelby herself. Like Eliza, Mrs. Shelby herself is a mother who has deep concerns for her family. In case Sam misunderstands her desires to let Eliza flee, Mrs. Shelby knowingly whispers to him not to ride the horses too fast. Sam smiles in agreement.

Andy and Sam derive much fun at Haley's expense. By rigging his horse to run wild, they get the better of the slave trader and effectively delay the pursuit. Through their conniving tricks and jokes, they obtain revenge on Haley for buying Shelby's slaves without risking Haley's or Mr. Shelby's retaliation. Ultimately, they know that Mrs. Shelby is on their side.

Study Questions

1. How does Mrs. Shelby find out that Eliza is missing?

2. What is Mr. and Mrs. Shelbys' reaction to the news of Eliza's escape?

3. Who is the only servant in the house who is not surprised?

4. What other information shocks the servants?

5. What is Sam's initial boast to Andy?

6. How does Andy caution Sam regarding the chase?

7. After Haley's horse bolts, what does Sam do?

8. After Sam catches Haley's horse, what does he advise?

9. How does Mrs. Shelby contribute to delaying the hunt?

10. What are Sam's and Andy's reaction to the success of their delay tactics?

Answers

1. Mrs. Shelby keeps ringing for Eliza's help, but receives no response. She is told by other servants that Eliza has run away.

2. Mrs. Shelby praises God. Mr. Shelby feels awkward since he knows Haley might suspect him of not fulfilling their bargain.

3. Aunt Chloe is not surprised because Eliza told her the escape plan the night before.

4. The news that Uncle Tom has been sold takes the other servants by surprise.

5. Sam boasts that he will be the one to catch Eliza.

6. Andy cautions Sam that Mrs. Shelby does not want Eliza caught. They fear and respect her desires more than Mr. Shelby's.

7. Sam chases after Haley's horse. He intentionally frightens the horse more by shouting and waving a palm leaf.

8. Sam advises Haley that the horse must be rubbed down and rested.

9. Mrs. Shelby invites Haley in for dinner.

10. Sam and Andy enjoy a good laugh while discussing their success.

Suggested Essay Topics

1. Discuss Andy's and Sam's loyalty to Mrs. Shelby. What does it say about their relationship to her?

2. Examine Haley's impressions of the situation. Why does he think that he is being played for a fool? When does he believe that circumstances are beyond his control?

Chapters 7 and 8

New Characters:

Mr. Symmes: *a man who helps Eliza and Harry escape*

Tom Loker: *a slave catcher and acquaintance of Haley's*

Marks: *a lawyer, Tom Loker's partner*

Summary

Eliza and Harry walk past the Shelby plantation's boundaries as the mother thinks about the life she is leaving behind. Eliza plans to head toward the Ohio River and cross it from Kentucky into Ohio, a free state. She assures a frightened Harry that she will not let anyone harm him. They eventually stop at a tavern to rest. Nearby, the river is clogged by ice, and the water is turbulent. Eliza asks the tavernkeeper if a ferryboat will come to take them across. She receives an uncertain answer since traveling on the river appears dangerous. Harry becomes too tired to move further, and falls asleep.

Back at the Shelby plantation, Haley is still waiting to start after Eliza and Harry. Despite Mrs. Shelby's promise to serve Haley dinner, Aunt Chloe takes her time cooking it. Chloe and other servants in the kitchen curse Haley and hope he suffers God's vengeance. Uncle Tom cautions them not to wish any evil on anyone, even Haley. Tom counsels forgiveness and tells them to pray for Haley's soul. Tom also understands Mr. Shelby's actions and will abide by his decision. As Tom explains, "Mas'r couldn't help hisself; he did right." Mrs. Shelby tells Tom that she will try to buy him back as soon as she can.

After dinner, Sam and Andy finally join Haley in their pursuit of the runaways. Haley decides to head toward the river, but Sam informs him that two roads lead in that direction. Sam and Andy can only guess as to which one Eliza had taken. Haley becomes suspicious of their game, not knowing for certain whether they lie or not. Sam is "in wonderful spirits," sounding false alarms on Eliza's appearance and "keeping Haley in a state of constant commotion."

After a while, however, the search party arrives at the tavern in which Eliza and Harry are resting. When Sam sees her before the others do, he distracts Haley while alerting Eliza of the searchers' presence. Eliza quickly grabs Harry and runs toward the river. She carries her son and jumps from one floating ice block to another, "stumbling—leaping—slipping—springing upwards again!" On the Ohio shore, Mr. Symmes, a kind acquaintance of the Shelbys', helps Eliza and Harry out of the water. Haley, Sam, and Andy can only watch in amazement at Eliza's bravery. Sam and Andy share a good laugh at Haley and ride back to the Shelby plantation, leaving the trader behind.

As Sam and Andy return to the plantation, Haley stops by the tavern in which Eliza and Harry had just been. Haley meets an acquaintance there, Tom Loker, a burly slave catcher with "a shaggy and fierce appearance." With Loker is his friend Marks, a lawyer who is "short and slender, lithe and cat-like in his motions." Haley tells them of his misfortune regarding the attempted capture of Eliza and Harry. The three then strike a deal among themselves. If Loker and Marks catch the fugitives, they will keep Eliza to sell for themselves. Haley would get back Harry.

At the Shelby plantation, Sam and Andy recount their side of the story. Mr. and Mrs. Shelby learn that Eliza and Harry have reached the apparent safety of Ohio. Sam and Andy retire to Chloe's kitchen to eat and tell of their adventures to the rest of the servants.

Analysis

In Chapter 7, Eliza is driven by her maternal love for Harry and braves crossing the dangerous river. Eliza and Harry, being mulattoes, or slaves of mixed parentage, are not suspected of being fugitives because they appear as almost white. Thus the tavernkeeper, or anyone else whom Eliza comes across, never questions her motives for escape. Stylistically, the author directly tries to arouse the reader's sympathy for Eliza's plight. Harriet Beecher Stowe addresses us by asking, "If it were your Harry, mother, or your Willie, that were going to be torn from you by a brutal trader,…how fast could you walk?" Whether for white or black, Stowe maintains that feelings of humanity and family must outweigh the material concerns of slavery. The author also employs suspense at dramatizing Eliza's running and jumping across the river, holding the reader's attention through the story's action.

At the Shelby plantation, Uncle Tom demonstrates his power of faith and forgiveness. While the other servants curse Haley, Tom pities the state of the trader's soul. Tom even forgives Mr. Shelby for selling him, knowing that his master is in financial trouble. Tom is willing to sacrifice himself for the good of the plantation. The theme of sacrifice is important here, and will appear again in the book. Tom can be considered as a Christ-like character. Like Christ, he is humble, pious, and forgiving. Tom is also willing to sacrifice his own comfort and his life for the sake of everyone else's.

As in Chapter 6, the author again resorts to humor when portraying Sam and Andy, who enjoy several hilarious moments at Haley's expense. They use all their wit and cunning to outfox the trader, leading him down false trails and intentionally misunderstanding him. Once again, Sam and Andy triumph over Haley in the end, laughing at the day's adventures.

Sam's and Andy's antics contribute to the theme of resistance vs. oppression. Although slaves must take orders or be punished, they also can devise ways of resisting their servile condition. Eliza decides on the most evident form of resistance by running away. Sam and Andy indirectly oppose Haley's wishes by pretending not to comprehend him. They also appear to be helpful, but intentionally make matters worse for the trader.

Mr. Symmes is introduced to the reader near the end of this chapter. After Eliza's daring escape across the river, he helps her with directions. Mr. Symmes is caught in an ambivalent situation because he knows Mr. Shelby, but is also aiding one of his slaves to run away. Uneasy, Mr. Symmes talks in dialect to himself: "Shelby, now, mebbe won't think this yer the most neighborly thing in the world; but what's a feller to do?" The issue of slavery constantly forces the characters to take a stand. Although neither educated nor religious, Mr. Symmes makes a moral judgment because of his overriding humanity to help Eliza.

In Chapter 8, the discussion that occurs among Tom Loker, Marks, and Haley presents their views on slavery as well as on their occupations. The description of Loker's face, which is "expressive

of brutal and unhesitating violence," personifies his whole character. In contrast, his friend Marks displays a "dry, cautious acuteness"
through a "thin and quivering voice." Despite their different personalities, both men complement one another and work well together.
As Marks approvingly states in dialect to his companion: "If you an't
the devil, Tom, you's his twin brother, I'll say that for ye!"

Haley provides a somewhat opposite view to that of his
acquaintances. He bemoans the loss of Harry and defiant slave
mothers like Eliza. However when Tom Loker tells of his own example of controlling slaves with threats of violence, Haley disagrees.
The trader wishes for something less brutal, saying "trade an't everything, and money an't everything, 'cause we's all got souls." Haley
cannot wholly abide by the wickedness of his profession, and announces that he will be more religious one of these days. Tom Loker
naturally despises Haley's posturing, emphasizing that Haley has
always been in league with the devil, only turning pious when
things go against him. Although they all engage willingly in slave
catching, Haley at least superficially yearns for something more
spiritually satisfying.

At the end of Chapter 8, Sam recounts Eliza's miraculous escape across the river, and Mrs. Shelby is relieved. Yet she feels great
remorse for Eliza's situation, claiming that the Shelbys have sinned
in their participation in slavery. Stowe uses sarcasm to point out
to the reader how slave catching, although morally wrong, is legally justified. As in the previous chapter, she again addresses us,
noting: "The catching business…is rising to the dignity of a lawful
and patriotic profession." This theme of law vs. religion will appear again later.

Study Questions

1. Why does Eliza take her time walking with Harry?

2. How does Aunt Chloe delay the preparation of dinner at the
   Shelbys?

3. How does Aunt Chloe react to Tom's advice to pray for Haley?

4. What is Tom's concern once he is taken away by Haley?

5. What does Mr. Shelby promise Haley?

6. What does Haley think is the hardest part of slave trading?

7. Describe Loker's and Marks's plans once they catch Eliza.

8. What does Haley request from the slavecatchers?

9. How does Sam explain the miracle of Eliza's escape across the river?

10. What does Aunt Chloe do for Sam upon his return?

Answers

1. She takes her time walking with her son so as not to attract anyone's notice that they are actually running away.

2. Aunt Chloe and her helpers cause numerous accidents in the kitchen to delay dinner.

3. Aunt Chloe says that she cannot pray for the trader's soul.

4. Tom is worried that the plantation will not be run as effectively once he is gone.

5. Mr. Shelby promises Haley that one thousand dollars will be paid to him if Tom runs away.

6. Haley believes that dealing with children is the most difficult part of his profession, mainly because their mothers put up a fight or flee.

7. Loker and Marks plan on taking Eliza to New Orleans and sell her to the highest bidder.

8. Haley wants a percentage of their profits once they sell Eliza. Loker and Marks refuse.

9. Sam says that Eliza's escape was helped by divine intervention.

10. Aunt Chloe cooks him a large meal.

Suggested Essay Topics

1. Discuss Tom's attitude toward Mr. Shelby, Haley, and the remaining servants. Which one(s) does he feel the most sorry for, and why?

2. Discuss the relationship between Tom Loker and Haley. What role does Marks play in their discussion?

3. Describe Sam's manner and style of telling the story of Eliza's escape. How does his rendition differ when he tells Mr. and Mrs. Shelby, and then to the other servants?

Chapter 9

New Characters:

Senator Bird: *a politician who supports the Fugitive Slave Law*

Mrs. Bird: *the Senator's pious wife*

John Van Trompe: *a neighbor of the Birds*

Summary

The scene changes to Senator and Mrs. Bird's home in Ohio. The Senator, a man who possesses "a particularly humane and accessible nature," has just returned from Washington, D.C. after a period of legislating. Mrs. Bird, a religious woman, questions her husband on the morals of passing the Fugitive Slave Law. She wonders how a supposedly Christian legislature could make laws that forbid assisting runaways. Her own Christian sense of morality leads Mrs. Bird to declare that she will break the law if she must. Senator Bird, who had supported the law while in Congress, explains that the statute had been passed to calm slave holders in Kentucky who feared losing their slaves to the North.

At this point, Eliza and Harry show up at the Birds' door. Tired and hungry from fleeing, Eliza tells the Birds of how she had crossed the ice-jammed river to escape from slave catchers. She also details some of her past situation: Mr. Shelby's debts, the threat of being separated from Harry, how her husband George also fled from his master.

Because of his humanity, Senator Bird decides to help Eliza and Harry on their journey to Canada. He takes them to his neighbor John Van Trompe, a former slave owner who now shelters fugitive slaves. Van Trompe promises to look after Eliza and Harry in the meantime.

Analysis

When Senator and Mrs. Bird discuss the Fugitive Slave Law, several important issues arise. One is the role of Mrs. Bird as a religious wife and mother influencing her husband. The Birds' conversation is similar to Mr. and Mrs. Shelby's earlier in the novel. Both talks between husband and wife focus on the women's argument against slavery on moral grounds. The husbands, however, can only see the practical sides of compromising on the topic. Mr. Shelby must sell his slaves to avoid financial disaster; Senator Bird has to support the law against fugitives to appease his fellow politicians. Both of their wives are defiant against the evils of slavery. In fact, Mrs. Bird declares about the law, "I'll break it...the first time I get a chance; and I hope I shall have a chance, I do!"

Stowe uses the theme of family to clarify the issue of slavery. At first, Senator Bird uses symbolic language. He explains to his wife, "we mustn't suffer our feelings to run away with our judgment." To the Senator, practical logic is only good if it metaphorically does not "run away," as slaves literally do. He argues that "public interests" must take priority over "private feelings." As a politician, he feels that he must take more into consideration than his wife thinks.

Mrs. Bird, however, gets the better of her husband by personalizing the argument. Here the theme of law vs. religion emerges again. Mrs. Bird asks her husband if he would, in accordance with the law, turn away any escaped slaves who appeared at their own home. Being a kind and conscience-stricken man, the Senator has trouble answering. He is later put to the test when Eliza and Harry do appear before him. The Senator also thinks about his own family, the Birds having a son who had died in infancy. When Eliza asks for their sympathy by pointing to her own son, the Birds relate to her concerns. The Senator finally votes for helping the fugitives, violating the very law that he had endorsed.

Stowe addresses the reader by emphasizing the irony of Senator Bird's situation. The author labels him "a political sinner" and "a sad case for his patriotism." In other words, the Senator had thought that he was doing the best for his country by patriotically supporting the Fugitive Slave Law. He morally sinned, however, by compromising in politics. At his wife's urging, the Senator saves his own soul by helping Eliza and Harry.

Senator Bird's neighbor, Van Trompe, had shared a similar circumstance. He had owned slaves, but later freed them under the influence of religion. Here and throughout the book, the theme of religion provides the motivating force for characters such as Van Trompe, Mrs. Shelby, and Mrs. Bird to debate against slavery.

Study Questions

1. What issue prompts Mrs. Bird to discuss politics with her husband?

2. What does Mrs. Bird call the Fugitive Slave Law?

3. Why does Senator Bird at first believe that the law is "right and Christian"?

4. What does Senator Bird suggest to his wife when they see Eliza and Harry?

5. How does Eliza gain the sympathy of Mrs. Bird?

6. What do the Birds give to Harry?

7. Why does Senator Bird want to move Eliza and Harry to Van Trompe's place?

8. Why does Senator Bird himself take them to Van Trompe's?

9. From where is Van Trompe originally?

10. What does Senator Bird give to Van Trompe to pass on to Eliza?

Answers

1. The Fugitive Slave Law prompts Mrs. Bird to discuss politics.

2. She calls it a "shameful, wicked, abominable law."

3. He believes that he must support the law as a public duty to the country.

4. He suggests that they give Eliza and Harry some clothes and blankets.

5. Eliza asks Mrs. Bird if she had ever lost a child.

6. They give Harry their dead son's clothes.

7. He thinks that Eliza and Harry will be safer with Van Trompe because the slave catchers are nearby.

8. The Senator is the only one who knows the back roads to take through a rainy night.

9. He is originally from Kentucky. He moved to Ohio after freeing his slaves.

10. He gives Van Trompe a ten-dollar bill to give later to Eliza.

Suggested Essay Topics

1. Describe the relationship between Senator and Mrs. Bird. How do they affect one another?

2. What sort of characteristics does Mrs. Bird identify with in Eliza? How does this affiliation help Eliza?

Chapter 10

Summary

The scene returns to Uncle Tom's cabin. Tom gets ready to be taken and sold by Haley. Tom accepts his fate, saying, "I'm in the Lord's hands." Aunt Chloe, however, expresses her anguish at the injustice of the situation and finds little comfort in religion. Mrs. Shelby stops by the cabin to let Tom know that she will try to buy him back as soon as possible.

Haley then arrives to seize Tom. As they leave the plantation, Master George rides up to say his goodbyes to Tom. Knowing how their son is attached to Tom, the Shelbys decide not to tell Master George of the trade while he is visiting friends. Master George, however, rides back to the plantation in time and gives Tom a dollar coin. The slave then kindly lectures the boy to behave and respect his parents. Although stopped by Tom from harming Haley, Master George promises that when he is grown, he will neither buy nor sell slaves.

Analysis

This chapter focuses on the breakup of Tom's family. Feelings of frustration and sadness, along with a certain helplessness in their situation, affect many of the slaves. Although Chloe is considered pious, she cannot find consolation in prayer and her husband's spiritual advice. The children are too young to be concerned at first, but start to cry when they see their unhappy parents. The other slaves gather to bid their sad farewells to Tom, who they respect as "a head servant and a Christian teacher."

The strain of Tom's departure shows among the Shelby family as well. When Mrs. Shelby visits Tom and Chloe in their cabin, Chloe initially greets Mrs. Shelby with hostility. This feeling vanishes later when Mrs. Shelby promises that she will do whatever is necessary to get Tom back. Mr. Shelby, because of his guilty conscience, is not even present on the plantation so that he "might not witness the unpleasant scenes" that he had started by selling Tom. Master George exchanges some threatening words with Haley, but is restrained from violence by Tom. Master George has learned the most from this lesson of slavery, and vows to have nothing to do with it.

The author resorts to many stylistic devices here. She sets the scene's mood in the chapter's opening description, in which the February morning is "gray and drizzling." Stowe uses a metaphor to describe the slaves' feelings, writing that their "downcast faces" are "images of mournful hearts." Dialect is prevalent throughout the chapter. For example, Chloe expresses her anger and frustration toward her husband's situation, saying "de Lord lets drefful things happen, sometimes. I don't seem to get no comfort dat way."

Stowe also emphasizes the irony of solely blaming traders like Haley for the evils of slavery. Haley admits that he is only a small part of the trading business. As he notes to Master George: "So long as your grand folks wants to buy men and women, I'm as good as they is." Haley implies that in every transaction, two parties are involved, one to buy and the other to sell. Haley's comment accusingly points to the Shelbys as half of the problem of slavery.

Study Questions

1. What chores are Chloe doing for Tom before he leaves?

2. What does Chloe think Mr. Shelby owes Tom?

3. Why does Mrs. Shelby believe that giving money to Tom is not worthwhile?

4. What does Haley do when he takes Tom?

5. What had Master George been doing before he says goodbye to Tom?

6. Where do Haley and Tom stop on their journey?

7. Where does George put the dollar coin that he gives to Tom?

8. What threat does George promise to Haley?

9. What is George ashamed of being?

10. What does Haley promise to Tom?

Answers

1. Chloe irons Tom's clothes and cooks the last supper for him.

2. She thinks that Mr. Shelby owes Tom his freedom after years of loyal service.

3. She believes that the money would only be taken from Tom.

4. He puts shackles around Tom's ankles.

5. George had been away visiting friends. He had not even been told that Tom was leaving and came across him by accident.

6. They stop at a blacksmith's shop so Haley can have Tom's handcuffs altered to fit better.

7. With a string looped through a hole in the coin, George hangs it around Tom's neck and underneath his shirt.

8. He promises to tell his parents how Tom is being treated. Naturally Haley treats it as an empty threat.

9. He is ashamed of being a Kentuckian.

10. He promises to treat Tom nicely if the slave does not try to run away.

Suggested Essay Topics

1. Describe how the Shelbys have failed Tom. What are the different reactions of Mr. Shelby, his wife, and Master George?

2. How does Tom address his family? The Shelbys? Haley?

Chapter 11

New Characters:

Mr. Wilson: *George Harris's former employer at the factory*

A drover: *a cattle driver who converses with Mr. Wilson*

Jim: *a slave who escapes with George Harris*

Summary

Mr. Wilson, who is now identified as the manufacturer who employed George Harris from Chapter 2, appears at a hotel bar room in Kentucky. An "honest drover," or cattle driver, converses with Mr. Wilson, showing him an advertisement notifying its readers that George Harris has escaped. The notice gives a description of George, offering a four hundred dollar reward for his capture or death. The drover recounts how he had freed his own slaves, noting that if treated humanely, they would work and live productively as humans should.

Moments later, a mysterious Spanish-looking gentleman and his servant enter the tavern. The gentleman, named Henry Butler, and Mr. Wilson exchange glances, apparently recognizing one another. When Butler invites Mr. Wilson to a confidential meeting, the gentleman reveals himself as George Harris in disguise. His servant Jim is really a fellow runaway slave.

George tells his former employer of his escape plans. Mr. Wilson, "a good-natured but extremely fidgety and cautious" person, attempts to talk George out of his scheme to flee to Ohio and then Canada. The manufacturer believes that the risks are too great for his friend. George, however, is determined to be free, and announces that he would risk death for his own liberty.

Analysis

The discussion between Mr. Wilson and George Harris is emotionally strained. It clearly sets George's anti–slavery viewpoint against Mr. Wilson's argument for patience and caution. Although Mr. Wilson is sympathetic to George's plight, he at first cannot fully take a stand against slavery. Only later is he finally convinced of George's reasons for fleeing.

Mr. Wilson initially attempts to dissuade George from escaping because he is afraid for George's safety. Mr. Wilson bases his logic on two foundations: the nation's laws, which forbid slaves from running away, and the Bible, which demands that slaves submit to their masters. Here the theme of law vs. religion arises, but Mr. Wilson attempts to use both legal and moral grounds to support his arguments rather than pitting them against one another.

George counters this reasoning by arguing against both law and religion. As a slave, George states that he has no country; he did not participate in the making of or consenting to its laws. Considered legally as property, he maintains no rights under the law. George then mocks the ideas behind the Declaration of Independence, implying that people in America are not created free and equal. On the religious issue, he admits that his wife Eliza is Christian, and he is trying to be pious. However, George can no longer endure his condition as a slave. He declares himself a human being, with every right to live freely as anyone else. He thus challenges the secular principles of the Declaration of Independence, and the religious message within the Bible.

The reader also learns that George had a pious sister who had been sold by their master. His father had been a white slave owner who sold George, along with the rest of his family. The repetition of the theme of breaking up families is evident here. George's bitterness is derived from a lack of family and the sin of slavery. He confesses that Mr. Wilson had been the first person to have shown him any kindness.

The author personalizes the theoretical arguments against slavery by having characters ask others to imagine themselves in the slaves' place. George Harris inquires of Mr. Wilson how he would feel if his family were taken hostage by Indians and made to hoe corn for their captors. To this scenario, Mr. Wilson cannot offer an answer, knowing how he cares for his own family.

Study Questions

1. How does George Harris use his appearance to pass as a gentleman?

2. What is ironic about the name that George assumes?

3. What Bible passage does Mr. Wilson quote to George?

4. With what example does George confront Mr. Wilson?

5. How does George convince Mr. Wilson that he is ready to risk escape and even death?

6. What ideas about government does George get from listening to Fourth of July speeches?

7. What did George's father do to his family?

8. Who encouraged George to read and write?

9. What country does George feel safe to call his own?

10. What last instructions does George leave for Mr. Wilson?

Answers

1. He has a light enough complexion to disguise himself as a Spanish gentleman.

2. He takes the name Henry Butler, the last name implying a servant.

3. He quotes, "Let every one abide in the condition in which he is called" to justify George's slave status.

4. George wants to know how Mr. Wilson would feel if Indians had carried the manufacturer away from his family and made to work for them. George imagines that Mr. Wilson would not be satisfied with his condition in life then.

5. George displays two pistols and a knife.

6. He says that governments "derive their just power from the consent of the governed."

7. George's father sold the entire family, including the mother and seven children.

8. Mr. Wilson encouraged George.

9. He calls Canada his country.

10. George leaves Mr. Wilson a pin that George had received as a gift from Eliza. If George fails to reach Canada, he would like Mr. Wilson to send Eliza the pin for him as a sign of his love.

Suggested Essay Topics

1. Describe Mr. Wilson's understanding and use of the nation's laws and the Bible to justify his arguments. Why does he really want to dissuade George from running away?

2. Discuss George's personal history and its effects on his views of slavery.

Chapter 12

New Characters:

Lucy: *a slave whom Haley buys*

Aunt Hagar and Albert: *mother and son separated when Haley buys the boy*

Summary

As Haley and Uncle Tom head toward Washington, D.C., Haley notices an advertisement for a slave auction and plans on buying more laborers to sell south. Haley examines several of the slaves before the auction begins and buys a boy, Albert, away from his mother, Aunt Hagar. Aunt Hagar pleads with Haley to buy her too, so that she can be with her son. But Haley refuses because he would lose money on the deal, growling that Hagar is "an old rack o' bones,—not worth her salt." The trader then takes his gang of slaves onto a riverboat, heading further south. Several white passengers comment on the presence of the slaves and converse on the nature of slavery itself.

While on the boat, Haley then acquires a woman, Lucy, and her child. A fellow passenger becomes interested in buying the boy and starts bartering with Haley. The trader agrees to sell the child, but only when the man nears his destination so that he can depart with his purchase before the mother finds out. When Lucy discovers that her child is missing and has been sold to someone no longer on the boat, she jumps overboard and drowns.

Analysis

This chapter portrays Haley at his worst. Despite voicing spiritual concerns earlier to Tom Loker, Haley is remorseless at the prospect of earning money from slave trading. His thoughts on Uncle Tom center on the slave's "length, and breadth, and height, and what he would sell for." The slave trader heartlessly separates Aunt Hagar and Albert. On the riverboat, Haley obtains Lucy and her child, having no problem with his conscience when he sells the boy to a stranger. When Haley discovers that Lucy in despair had drowned herself, he grudgingly records the financial loss in his account book.

Haley's actions draw several responses from the passengers on the boat. Some defend slavery, concluding that slaves are leading better lives than if they were free. One even quotes a Bible passage as proof that blacks should be servants. On the other hand, others vehemently disapprove of the institution, citing the breakup of families, the ill treatment of slaves, and the sinfulness of the overall practice. The author clearly sides with this latter group by inspiring the reader's sympathy for slave mothers like Lucy, who have their children taken from them and sold.

At the end of the chapter, Stowe addresses the reader through the theme of individual vs. societal responsibility. She asks, "who...makes the trader? Who is most to blame?" Rather than fully denouncing the trader, Stowe also holds responsible those who directly or indirectly support the slave system. Anyone arguing for its defense, like some of the riverboat passengers, or who themselves buy slaves, are equally to blame. The author accuses Northerners as much as Southerners in their participation in the slave trade. Stowe resorts to sarcasm, writing: "The trader had arrived at that stage of Christian and political perfection which has been recommended by some preachers and politicians of the north." By this statement, she condemns the purely practical reasons that legal and moral institutions use for supporting slavery.

Study Questions

1. Where do Haley and Uncle Tom stay while in Washington, D.C.?

2. What does Aunt Hagar promise to Haley if he buys her together with her son?

3. What is Albert's special relationship to his mother?

4. Which passenger on the riverboat quotes the Bible to defend slavery?

5. Which passenger comments adversely on slavery and questions Haley?

6. How does Haley defend his position as a trader?

7. What makes some passengers think more about the horrors of slavery?

8. Why does Haley sell Lucy's child to the stranger?

9. Who first discovers that Lucy has jumped overboard?

10. How does Haley feel about the loss of Lucy?

Answers

1. Haley stays at a tavern; Tom is locked in a jail.

2. She promises that she is able to work hard on a plantation, despite being old and crippled.

3. Albert is Hagar's last son to be sold from her.

4. A minister recites the Bible passage.

5. A humane slave owner attacks slavery.

6. Haley says: "I took up the trade just to make a living."

7. Thinking about their own families, some passengers realize how terrible it is for slaves to be separated from their kin.

8. Haley thinks the child will decrease Lucy's value on the market because a plantation owner may not want the added financial burden of raising the child.

9. Uncle Tom notices during the night that Lucy drowns herself by seeing her run down the boat and hearing the splash in the water.

10. He feels "devilish unlucky."

Suggested Essay Topics

1. Describe some of the riverboat passengers' reactions to Haley in particular and slavery in general. How do they justify their arguments for or against slavery?

2. Discuss Haley's reasons and emotions for trading slaves. How does he explain his position from a personal perspective? From a religious perspective?

Chapter 13

New Characters:

Simeon and Rachel Halliday: *a Quaker couple who aid the Harris family*

Ruth Stedman: *a Quaker friend of the Hallidays'*

Summary

Eliza and Harry rest at the Quaker home of Simeon and Rachel Halliday, having been directed there by Van Trompe. A neighbor in the Quaker settlement, Ruth Stedman, visits the Hallidays and chats about the happenings in their community. Later, Simeon arrives with news that several other Quakers are bringing fugitives to the settlement, one of whom is Eliza's husband, George Harris. Eliza faints when she receives this information, waking later to find George at her bedside. The next day, the Quakers help the Harrises make plans to escape to Canada.

Analysis

Simeon and Rachel Halliday, as well as their friend Ruth Stedman, live by the Christian principle of doing good for others. Experienced in helping fugitives, the Quakers take in Eliza and her child and attempt to calm her fears. The Quakers do not judge or condemn anyone's character or motives. Simeon even says: "I would do...the same for the slave holder as for the slave, if the Lord brought him to my door in affliction." Clearly, the Hallidays side with the plight of the Harrises, but the Quakers' beliefs hold them to treat all with love and respect.

At first, Eliza and George feel uncomfortable in this environment. As escaped slaves, they are used to more uncertain and frightful times. George initially feels "constraint and awkwardness" when he sits at the Hallidays' breakfast table, never before having "sat down on equal terms at a white man's table." The Harrises, however, begin to feel at home with the Quakers, and are grateful for their kindness.

The author sets the mood of warmth and security in the Hallidays' home, writing that it possesses "an atmosphere of mutual confidence and good fellowship everywhere." She also highlights the theme of family and religion. The Quaker settlement, in which the Harris family reunites, characterizes the ideal blend of communal harmony and spirituality wherein each member of the family and the whole community treat one another with respect according to Christian morals.

Stowe uses a metaphor to describe Eliza, who has "grown under the discipline of heavy sorrow." To comfort Eliza, Rachel Halliday talks in Quaker dialect, saying: "Thee knows thee can stay here, as long as thee pleases."

Study Questions

1. What does Rachel Halliday ask about Eliza's plans?
2. What does Rachel offer Eliza?
3. Why does Eliza decline Rachel's offer?
4. What does Ruth Stedman bring for Harry?
5. To whom does Simeon Halliday first tell the news of George Harris' arrival?

6. Who tells Eliza the news of her husband's coming?

7. What does Eliza dream about during her fainting spell?

8. What must Simeon do if he is caught helping the Harrises escape?

9. What does George worry about regarding the Hallidays?

10. What does Simeon advise George to do regarding the escape plans?

Answers

1. Rachel would like to know what Eliza will do once she reaches Canada. As of yet, Eliza does not know.

2. Rachel offers her the hospitality of the Halliday home as long as Eliza desires.

3. Eliza declines the generosity because she feels unsafe in Ohio when the slave catchers are still looking for her and Harry.

4. She brings him a cake.

5. He first tells Rachel and Ruth.

6. Rachel tells Eliza the news.

7. Eliza dreams of her family being together at a home by the sea.

8. He must pay a fine.

9. He worries that the Hallidays are risking too much to aid him and his family.

10. He advises George to wait until nighttime to travel. Simeon assures George of the Quaker settlement's safety during the daytime.

Suggested Essay Topics

1. Describe the relationships among the Quaker settlement. What principles do they follow? How do these beliefs affect escaped slaves?

2. How do George and Eliza react to the Hallidays' generosity? Does it relieve the Harrises' worries? Why or why not?

Chapters 14 and 15

New Characters:

Augustine St. Clare: *a slave owner in New Orleans who buys Uncle Tom*

Marie: *St. Clare's selfish wife*

Eva: *the St. Clares' angelic daughter*

Miss Ophelia: *St. Clare's cousin from Vermont*

Adolph: *St. Clare's haughty servant*

Mammy: *another family servant*

Summary

Chapters 14 and 15 return to the plight of Uncle Tom. As the riverboat continues down the Mississippi River, Tom's goodwill wins the confidence of Haley. The slave trader unchains Tom, leaving him free to walk around. Occasionally, Tom even helps the boat crew with its chores. The pious slave also thinks of his family, trying to find comfort in his Bible.

On the boat, three passengers are introduced: Augustine St. Clare, his five-year-old daughter Eva, and Miss Ophelia, St. Clare's cousin from Vermont. Eva is "the perfection of childish beauty" and "something almost divine" with "long golden-brown hair." Tom is immediately taken with her, and they become fast friends, leading Eva to promise Tom that her father will purchase him. When she accidentally falls overboard, Tom rescues her.

St. Clare is a New Orleans gentleman who wears "a proud and somewhat sarcastic expression." He barters with Haley over the purchase of Tom, teasing and mocking the slave trader by suggesting that Tom's valued piousness and intelligence would only cause him trouble. Eventually, St. Clare buys Tom at Little Eva's prompting. Much of St. Clare's personal history is given. His father had been a rich Louisiana planter. St. Clare grew up with a sensitive character, having been influenced by his religious mother. He had been in love with a woman, but from misunderstandings, married instead Marie, his present wife. Marie, who is at New Orleans, possesses "a most intense and unconscious selfishness." St. Clare is

closely attached to his daughter Eva because she reminds him of his departed mother.

Miss Ophelia is from the New England branch of the St. Clare family. A 45-year-old spinster who is efficient, dutiful, and religious, she travels to New Orleans with her cousin and niece to help them run the household because Marie feels too ill to manage.

Landing at New Orleans, the party then proceeds to the St. Clare mansion and is greeted by Adolph, St. Clare's haughty servant. Tom is impressed by the calm and beauty of the place, but receives a cold response from Adolph. When Eva runs to hug and kiss Mammy, one of the servants, Miss Ophelia expresses her disgust and prejudice at the affectionate display. St. Clare then greets his wife, Marie, who is unappreciative of the gifts her husband brings. Upon meeting Tom, who will be her coachman, Marie declares that he will probably get drunk and be of little use to her.

Analysis

These chapters introduce Tom's new acquaintances and owners, the St. Clares. While on the riverboat, Eva and Tom take a fancy toward one another. Both are characterized as spiritual. The reader senses that Eva is sympathetic to the slaves' condition, as she becomes sorrowful at the sight of Haley's gang in chains. Because of her saintly nature, Eva's humanity is never in doubt. When St. Clare asks his daughter why she wants to buy Tom, she responds, "I want to make him happy." This statement characterizes the Christian ethic of doing good for others, as the Quakers had accomplished for the Harrises in the book's earlier chapters.

St. Clare and Miss Ophelia provide contrasting temperaments. St. Clare is proud, sarcastic, good-humored, humane, and leisurely. Miss Ophelia is regimented, organized, and determined, which inspires her to help run the St. Clare household. Although the two possess opposite personalities, they are fond of each other. Miss Ophelia had taken care of St. Clare when he was a boy, and her affection for him verges on the motherly. The two characters also display ambivalence. Although St. Clare owns slaves, he knows slavery is wrong. While Miss Ophelia is an anti–slavery Northerner, she has prejudices against blacks. Their characters will be developed in the later chapters.

Because of her own selfishness, Marie believes that her family is uncaring toward her needs. When St. Clare presents Tom to his wife, she declares that the new servant will get drunk despite his religious beliefs. When Eva tries to hug and kiss her mother, Marie worries about her own headache. Her whiny attitude affects the other characters adversely. The reader gets a hint that Marie contributes to St. Clare's tragic situation through their unhappy marriage.

Throughout these chapters, the author relies on several stylistic devices. Stowe portrays the Mississippi River as a metaphor for human activity: "Those turbid waters, hurrying, foaming, tearing along, [are] an apt resemblance of that headlong tide of business." She uses a simile to describe Eva. As Tom is reading his Bible, she appears to him as "one of the angels stepped out of his New Testament." Miss Ophelia is depicted as "a living impersonation of order, method, and exactness." Stowe employs other similes to portray the grounds on St. Clare's mansion, writing that a pond contains fish swimming in it "like so many living jewels" and the grass is "smooth as green velvet."

The author utilizes sarcastic humor to develop St. Clare's character. When St. Clare bargains with Haley over Tom's price, the slave trader promotes Tom as intelligent, but St. Clare pretends disinterest, saying that smart slaves run off or cause too much trouble. When Haley calls attention to Tom's piousness, St. Clare jokingly ponders about using Tom as a chaplain instead of a servant.

Study Questions

1. What makes Tom think of his old home in Kentucky?
2. How does Tom first attract Eva's attention?
3. Why does St. Clare kid Haley about Tom's piousness?
4. Why is Tom offended when St. Clare buys him?
5. From where did the St. Clare family originate?
6. Which of his parents does St. Clare take after?
7. What event reawakens St. Clare's tenderness and interest in his marriage?
8. What does Miss Ophelia consider the "great sin of sins"?

9. What gifts does St. Clare bring to his wife?

10. What does Miss Ophelia prescribe as a cure for Marie's headache?

Answers

1. Tom sees other slaves on other plantations as he passes by on the riverboat.

2. He makes her toys out of cherry stones and hickory nuts.

3. St. Clare believes that enough pious politicians have already ruined the country.

4. St. Clare warns him that Tom may be allowed to be drunk only once a week. Tom is hurt by this comment because he does not drink at all.

5. They originated from Canada. One side traveled south to Louisiana (where St. Clare's family lives), and one to Vermont (Miss Ophelia's side of the family).

6. St. Clare takes after his mother.

7. The birth of Eva reawakens St. Clare's passion.

8. She considers "shiftlessness," or laziness, as the greatest sin.

9. He gives Marie a picture of himself and Eva, as well as Tom to serve as her coachman.

10. She prescribes juniper berry tea.

Suggested Essay Topics

1. Describe St. Clare's bargaining methods with Haley. What points does St. Clare raise in regard to slavery? To religion?

2. Analyze Miss Ophelia's perception of the world. How does the New England region affect her views?

3. In what ways are Uncle Tom and Eva alike?

Chapter 16

Summary

St. Clare, Marie, and Miss Ophelia discuss the nature of slavery and religion in this chapter. At first, Marie complains about how people, especially her servants, are inattentive to her concerns. She also believes that her husband fits this uncaring category and calls Eva "peculiar" for wanting to help others, including the servants.

St. Clare states that servants sometimes cannot help their behavior, given the circumstances that they face in slavery. When Miss Ophelia says that slave owners have a responsibility to their servants, St. Clare cites Northerners' prejudice against blacks despite denouncing the Southerners' ill treatment of slaves. When Marie enjoys a church sermon that defends slavery, St. Clare is quick to criticize the uses to which religion is put. St. Clare announces that Eva is the "only true democrat," caring for everyone equally regardless of race or social condition.

Analysis

The nature of slavery is addressed here in various ways. Despite Marie's views that servants are already lazy and spoiled, St. Clare believes that slaves behave in certain ways because of the surrounding conditions in which they exist. He thinks it unfair for owners to "make the fault and punish it too." By this, he hints that slavery is inefficient as a labor system because it is forced upon unwilling participants. Therefore, one cannot brand slaves as lazy and punish them for it. St. Clare also distrusts the religious support of slavery, viewing it as unreasonable. He suggests that if cotton prices declined and the need for slavery decreased as well, sermons would justify the abolishment of slavery.

When Miss Ophelia adds her opinions to the topic, the issues become more complicated. She believes that slaves have souls as well as white people, and that masters have a responsibility to educate their servants. However, St. Clare cuts through this self-righteous stance. He accuses Northerners like Miss Ophelia of personally disdaining black people while trying to help them, saying: "You loathe them as you would a snake or a toad, yet you are indignant of their wrongs." Miss Ophelia admits the partial truth in this statement.

In response, Ophelia attempts to force St. Clare to clarify his views on slavery, asking him "do you think slavery right or wrong?" Her cousin dodges this question by refusing to answer it because he is aware of his own ambivalent position. Like Mr. Shelby earlier, St. Clare is a humane slave holder. He buys slaves as if they were property, but treats them as family members. Either way that St. Clare responds to Ophelia's question, he knows that she will "be at me with half a dozen others, each one harder than the last."

The views of Marie St. Clare fit the theme of self-delusion. Marie personifies this trait in her selfishness and failure to understand other people's motivations. Despite Eva's or St. Clare's kindness toward her, Marie still abides by the notion that no one actually cares for her. However, Marie is the person who is uncaring toward others. As she tells Miss Ophelia about slavery in the South, "it's we mistresses that are the slaves, down here." None of the other characters, however, can take this statement seriously, given the conditions of the servants' lives. St. Clare responds with sarcastic comments to his wife, while Miss Ophelia maintains a baffled silence, not knowing how to react to such opinions.

Study Questions

1. Why does St. Clare tell Marie that her chores and worries will lessen?

2. In what ways does Marie think that her servants are spoiled?

3. Why does Marie believe that her daughter Eva is peculiar?

4. What does Marie criticize about her husband's treatment of the servants?

5. Despite her silence at Marie's talks about the servants, how does Miss Ophelia really feel about St. Clare's wife?

6. How does Ophelia react when she sees Eva embracing Uncle Tom?

7. What is Uncle Tom's job at the St. Clare residence when he is not the coachman?

8. What explanation does St. Clare give for not attending church services?

9. What advice does Marie give to Eva regarding the servants?

10. What does Uncle Tom wish for St. Clare?

Answers

1. He tells Marie that Ophelia will run the household for them.

2. She thinks that they are spoiled because they wear fine clothes and eat well, but are inattentive to her needs.

3. She thinks that her daughter is peculiar because Eva puts herself on equal terms with everyone, including servants.

4. She criticizes St. Clare for being too lenient with them. He disallows any beating of the servants.

5. Ophelia is aghast at Marie's opinions.

6. She reacts with horror, despite her anti–slavery feelings.

7. He is Eva's personal servant.

8. He states that attending church makes him fall asleep.

9. She tells Eva that servants should be treated properly, but not as family members.

10. Tom hopes that St. Clare will be converted to Christianity.

Suggested Essay Topics

1. What sort of relationship do St. Clare and Marie have? On what do they agree or disagree?

2. Describe why Eva is the "only true democrat." How does this title conform to her religious beliefs?

3. How does Miss Ophelia view slavery? What prompts her opinions of servants?

Chapter 17

New Character:

Phineas Fletcher: *a Quaker neighbor of the Hallidays' who helps the Harris family escape*

Summary

This chapter returns to the Hallidays' home, with George and Eliza Harris making plans on what they might do once they reach Canada. Simeon Halliday introduces them to his friend Phineas Fletcher, a "hearty, two-fisted backwoodsman" who married a Quaker woman and joined the settlement. Phineas brings news that slave catchers are nearby, and with his guidance, the escaped slaves head out. Included in their party is Jim, who earlier had run away with George, and Jim's mother.

As the group travels along during the night, Tom Loker and his gang spot it, and a chase ensues. The fugitives and Phineas hide behind some rocks on a steep hill. Tom Loker climbs after them, but is shot and wounded by George and pushed back down the hill by Phineas. Marks, Tom Loker's partner, leads the hurried retreat from the scene and leaves Loker behind. George and the others take pity on the slave catcher and decides to bring him to a Quaker home for nursing.

Analysis

The Harris family still take refuge among their Quaker friends. Although George hopefully ponders about his family's future in Canada, Eliza cautions him that they are not yet out of danger. When Phineas Fletcher visits the Hallidays, he only confirms Eliza's fears by reporting that Tom Loker and his search party are close. Phineas had earlier stopped by a tavern in which he had seen and overheard Loker's men discuss the escaped slaves.

This section focuses mainly on George's search for freedom and Christian faith. Throughout hearing Phineas Fletcher's news, George gets discouraged, bitterly asking, "Is God on our side?...Why does he let such things happen?" George cannot abide by the appearance that lawmakers, churchmen, and the wealthy seem to

be favored with the power to determine others' fates, especially slaves'. Simeon Halliday, however, convinces him otherwise. As the Quaker wisely counsels, "it is often those who have least of all in this life whom he chooseth for the kingdom." This statement, alongside of Simeon's own example of risking his life to help slaves, provides a religious perspective that comforts George. George promises his wife: "I'll try to act worthy of a free man. I'll try to feel like a Christian."

George is set on gaining his freedom, even if he must resort to violence. As he challenges the slave catchers: "I'm a free man, standing on God's free soil." Stowe connects this statement to the Declaration of Independence's rhetoric of liberty and equality. She writes: "George stood out in fair sight, on top of the rock, as he made his declaration of independence." As a human being, George claims his right to live as freely as white people by adapting ideas taken from the American Revolution.

The theme of law vs. morality appears in this chapter. When Tom Loker's gang approaches the fugitives' hideaway, one of them declares: "You see, we're officers of justice. We've got the law on our side, and the power, and so forth." The author maintains, however, that the law does not necessarily equate with moral justice, but with the power to oppress slaves.

Phineas Fletcher supports George's actions by shoving Tom Loker down the hill. Although a Quaker professing nonviolence, Phineas still has enough of his old habits left in him to relish a good fight. Once the group sees Loker in his helplessly wounded state, however, they have compassion on the slave catcher, aiding him when his own companions have abandoned him. Phineas and the escaped slaves thus display a consistent sense of humanity with their religious beliefs, providing a better example than the slave catchers who profess legal justice.

Study Questions

1. What occupation does Eliza hope to pursue when she gets to Canada?

2. What does George plan on doing for his master and Mr. Shelby?

3. What does George bring out when he hears the news of slave catchers being nearby?

4. Why does Phineas go along with the party of escaped slaves?

5. At what sport does Phineas excel?

6. What does Ruth Stedman bring for the Harris family?

7. Who fires the first shot at George?

8. Why do the slave catchers leave Tom Loker?

9. When Phineas binds Loker's wounds, who does the slave catcher mistake him for?

10. What do Eliza and Jim's mother worry about regarding Tom Loker?

Answers

1. She hopes to become a dressmaker.

2. He plans on paying them back for the losses caused by his and Eliza's running away.

3. He brings out his pistols.

4. He accompanies them because he knows the roads.

5. He excels at hunting deer.

6. Ruth brings some woolen socks for them to wear during the Canadian winters.

7. Marks, Tom Loker's partner, fires at George, but misses.

8. They leave him because he is too heavy to carry on horseback.

9. Loker thinks that Phineas is Marks.

10. They worry about the state of Loker's sinful soul and God's judgment upon it.

Suggested Essay Topics

1. Discuss Simeon Halliday's and Phineas Fletcher's views on violence. What do they advise George to do?

2. In what ways does Phineas's former life as a backwoodsman help the fugitives?

🖎 Chapters 18 and 19

New Characters:

Old Dinah: *the St. Clares' cook*

Prue: *an old slave at a neighboring house*

Jane and Rosa: *some other of St. Clare's haughty servants*

Summary

As time passes at the St. Clare house, Uncle Tom earns St. Clare's trust and confidence. Since St. Clare is described as "indolent and careless of money," he begins to rely on Tom to take charge of everyday business matters such as marketing. Adolph, St. Clare's personal servant, is just as heedless as his master, and he grows jealous of Tom's success within the household. When St. Clare comes home drunk late one evening, Tom tearfully implores him the next morning to look after his own soul. St. Clare is touched by Tom's concern and swears not to indulge in drunken revelries again.

Chapter 18 then turns to Miss Ophelia and her daunting task of putting the St. Clare mansion in order. Going through cabinets, cupboards, and closets, Ophelia organizes the place, much to the shock and curiosity of the servants. One who protests this "vigorous onslaught" is Old Dinah, the head cook for the St. Clares. She resents Ophelia's intrusion upon her realm of influence, the kitchen. In frustration, St. Clare's cousin can only respond, "Such shiftless management, such waste, such confusion, I never saw!" St. Clare defends Dinah's methods because she makes delicious meals in spite of the disorder.

When Ophelia complains of the waste and dishonesty of the servants, St. Clare remains unfazed. He notes that under the conditions of slavery, servants understandingly have no use for honesty. To them, the concept of stealing does not exist since they themselves are considered property. St. Clare is also unconcerned with their spiritual state or their education, despite Ophelia's admonition that he should be more responsible toward his servants.

Prue, a downhearted slave from nearby, stops to talk to Old Dinah. Prue wishes that she were dead to escape from her misery. Some of St. Clare's haughty slaves like Adolph, Jane, and Rosa tease her, emphasizing that Prue gets drunk too much. Uncle Tom tries to tell Prue about Christianity and wishes that she would stop drinking. Prue explains how she once had a child, but it had died from starvation, and now only sadness and alcohol remain for her.

In Chapter 19, Miss Ophelia and St. Clare continue their discussion on slavery when they learn about the death of Prue. The news spreads throughout the house when Prue fails to show in Dinah's kitchen. The St. Clare servants later hear that Prue had been put in a cellar and whipped to death because of her drunkenness.

St. Clare reacts nonchalantly, saying, "I thought it would come to that, some time." To Miss Ophelia's horror, he explains that because slaves are considered property in the eyes of the law, no protection exists for them. "Irresponsible despots," St. Clare notes, "have absolute control," and nothing he could do would change the situation. If masters choose to treat their possessions in this manner, he asks Ophelia, "what can a man of honorable and humane feelings do, but shut his eyes all he can, and harden his heart?" St. Clare also points out that slavery is defended by the clergy, his fellow planters, and politicians, who all can quote the Bible or some other source to justify the system.

St. Clare then delves into more of his family history, explaining to Ophelia how he had become enmeshed in the slavery business. He had inherited his servants from his father, who had moved from New England to Louisiana to become a planter. At his father's death, St. Clare and his twin brother Alfred divided the estate. Since St. Clare had no talent for running the family plantation, Albert took it over and St. Clare received the New Orleans mansion. He had thought earlier about doing something to reform society, "more than to float and drift." However, St. Clare lost any initiative other than to live life easily. He did not free his slaves because he was used to having them. At the dinner table, St. Clare tells his family of the time when he motivated a slave named Scipio through kindness when no one else could.

The chapter closes with Uncle Tom attempting to write a letter to his family in Kentucky. Little Eva tries to help, but neither are very successful. Out of pity, St. Clare offers to write to Tom's family for him, even though St. Clare disbelieves the Shelbys' promise to buy Tom back.

Analysis

The reader obtains a more developed sense of St. Clare's and Miss Ophelia's characters and opinions in these chapters. Chapter 18 depicts St. Clare as a gentleman of leisure who is not particularly desirous of putting much effort into anything. He provides a consistent example for his servants by not requiring them to labor too hard, thinking it "easier to indulge than to regulate." He spends no time on their education because he believes "a training of his servants was unjust and dangerous." St. Clare is not a churchgoer, instead spending his time attending dinner parties and other festivities. Uncle Tom, with his devout habits, at first only confuses his master. St. Clare vows to reform himself, however, because Tom presents a type of caring and responsible servant with whom St. Clare is unfamiliar yet influenced by.

Miss Ophelia challenges St. Clare's notions about the role of servants and household upkeeping. As described previously, Ophelia is systematic and to the point. Old Dinah, the head cook, is used to St. Clare's neglectful ways and runs the kitchen according to her own "opinionated and erratic" methods. The two come into conflict when Ophelia tries to impose her outlook onto Dinah. The situation is tense but humorous. Dinah obviously refuses to abide by Ophelia's dictates, but does so by remaining inattentive to Ophelia's suggestions.

Ophelia expresses her frustrations to St. Clare, and they debate the purposes and conditions of slavery. Ophelia believes that the servants are lazy and dishonest, and she is bothered by "the waste,—the expense!" St. Clare in turn answers that the conditions of slavery do not motivate servants to be efficient since they themselves have little to gain from it. St. Clare attempts to be neither for nor against slavery, but merely to live by the reality of what already exists within the institution. He sees no need to tend to his servants' souls because he himself is unbelieving. As he candidly states: "The fact is, the whole race are pretty generally understood to be turned over to the devil, for our benefit." Ophelia is shocked by this view, but St. Clare points to other examples in the world in which those in power have taken advantage of others.

The theme of dehumanization is characterized through Prue. Working under a harsh and unfeeling mistress, Prue declares in dialect, "I wish't I's dead!" She drinks frequently to "forget my misery." St. Clare's servants make fun of Prue because they live under the benevolent rule of a humane master and do not understand her situation. In certain ways, Prue confirms St. Clare's implications about slavery in that it provides no motivation for servants to labor well. In fact, Prue's circumstances go beyond St. Clare's observations because slavery actually dehumanizes people.

The repetition of this theme occurs earlier when George Harris wishes that he had never been born. He fears losing his wife and child and cannot bear his brutal master. Prue recounts her past to Uncle Tom about how she had lost her child. Tom then understands why Prue behaves the way she does, suffering because of slavery's unfairness and severity, and not because she is a bad or lazy person.

Although Chapter 19 depicts Miss Ophelia's and St. Clare's conversation on slavery, it focuses more on St. Clare's views than on his cousin's. The reader learns about St. Clare's personal history, and how he developed his attitudes toward slavery and the overall concept of labor. Prue's death ignites Ophelia's moral outrage, and she cannot understand St. Clare's coldhearted stance on this issue. St. Clare continually defends his own participation in possessing slaves by comparing the plantation system to other forms of labor. American planters, he suggests, are similar to the English capitalists; each take advantage of those less fortunate than they. The laborer in both systems ends up being exploited. As he explains: "The slave-owner can whip his refractory slave to death,—the capitalist can starve him to death." Either way, the results are gruesome for the worker.

St. Clare also takes Ophelia to task on her self-righteousness. Northerners, he claims, are not much different from their Southern brethren. He uses the St. Clare family itself as his example. The New England St. Clares are considered democratic while the Louisiana branch is labeled aristocratic. Yet Ophelia's father in Vermont is similar to St. Clare's, both having "that same strong, overbearing, dominant spirit" that is capable of oppressing the less fortunate.

From this discussion, Stowe characterizes her attacks on both Northerners and Southerners for their stance on slavery through St. Clare and Miss Ophelia. Both characters represent the ambivalence surrounding the slavery argument. Miss Ophelia thinks that slavery is inhumane and unchristian, taking the moral high ground on the issue. However, she also displays personal prejudices against blacks, calling them lazy, dishonest, and wasteful. Earlier, in Chapter 15, she is repulsed that Eva hugs and caresses Mammy, the family servant. St. Clare realizes the ethical problems of holding slaves, and criticizes the hypocrisy of religious people for supporting slavery, as well as abolitionists with prejudices like Ophelia. Yet he cannot move himself to free any of his slaves, let alone have the courage to speak out against the practice.

The only person who expresses dissatisfaction with all of these viewpoints is Eva. She listens to some of the adults' conversation and with a simple directness, she sadly and metaphorically concludes, "these things sink into my heart." Eva repeats this statement at the beginning of this chapter when she learns about Prue's death. Only Eva, through her pious innocence, acknowledges the true sin and sadness of slavery.

Study Questions

1. What does Tom say to make St. Clare stop drinking?

2. What is Old Dinah's rule to live by in the kitchen?

3. What does Prue bring with her to sell?

4. What does Miss Ophelia think about Prue and her habits?

5. When Uncle Tom tells Prue about heaven, why does she think that she will hate it there?

6. What reason does St. Clare give as a defense against whipping a slave to death?

7. What has St. Clare been tempted to do when he seriously thinks about the effects of slavery, especially on children?

8. What does St. Clare point to in New England that makes that region less righteous in its stance against slavery?

9. Why does Miss Ophelia think that St. Clare's comparison of American slave holders to English capitalists is inaccurate?

10. What does St. Clare predict will happen sooner or later with the slaves and other workers in the world?

Answers

1. Tom says that St. Clare has been kind to everyone except to himself, and that St. Clare should look after his own body and soul.

2. Her rule is that "the cook can do no wrong."

3. Prue brings along some rusks, or biscuits, to sell.

4. She calls Prue "very wicked and very foolish."

5. Prue thinks that she will not like heaven because her hard master and other white people will be there.

6. He states that masters should have an interest in maintaining their property, and slaves fall under this category.

7. He is tempted to curse his country and the whole human race.

8. St. Clare's father and an overseer on the father's plantation were from Vermont. These people were thus involved directly in the business of slavery.

9. She thinks that St. Clare's comparison is inaccurate because English capitalists do not sell families away from each other or whip them to death.

10. He predicts that a mass revolution will occur.

Suggested Essay Topics

1. Compare and contrast St. Clare's and Miss Ophelia's views on the role of servants. For what does Ophelia think that masters should be responsible?

2. Discuss how St. Clare became a slave holder and Miss Ophelia a slavery opponent. How did their family backgrounds affect their views?

3. Examine St. Clare's opinions on slavery. Is he being realistic or unsympathetic? How do these descriptions coincide with St. Clare being a humane slave holder?

Chapter 20

New Character:

Topsy: *eight or nine-year-old slave girl whom St. Clare purchases*

Summary

St. Clare decides to put his and Miss Ophelia's ideas about slavery to the test. He buys Topsy, a slave girl, for Ophelia to raise and educate. Topsy's expression is "an odd mixture of shrewdness and cunning" and "the most doleful gravity and solemnity." At first, Ophelia protests that she has no use for Topsy, being also repulsed by the slave girl. St. Clare, however, is quick to point out the hypocrisy of Christians like Ophelia, who willingly send missionaries overseas, but refuse to help and reform blacks in their own homes. St. Clare also recounts some of Topsy's past, in which she had been constantly beaten by her drunken masters.

Ophelia halfheartedly accepts her cousin's challenge to make something out of Topsy. Ophelia's task is made more difficult by the other servants' disdainful attitudes toward the new slave girl. Ophelia is then left with the sole responsibility of raising Topsy. She begins by asking Topsy several questions about the girl's life. Topsy, however, cannot tell who her parents were or how old she is. Having been raised by slave traders to sell on the market, Topsy's education is severely lacking. When Ophelia inquires of the girl's parents, Topsy answers, "Never was born!"

Ophelia begins Topsy's education with homemaking skills, as well as reading and religious instruction. When Ophelia catches her stealing some gloves and ribbon, Topsy initially denies any wrongdoing. She then confesses to the crime, but also proceeds to

confess to other incidents that she did not commit. Ophelia becomes exasperated at the child's behavior, not knowing whether
Topsy tells truths or lies. Eva tries to say something kind to Topsy,
but the slave girl laughs at the attempts.

Ophelia fears that she can no longer avoid whipping Topsy for
her bad behavior. St. Clare, upon hearing Ophelia's complaints and
frustrations, ponders again over the nature of slavery. He suggests
to his cousin that her experiences are much like the Southern slave
holder's in that they must resort to physical punishment. Both
masters and slaves become adversely affected by this system. As
he observes, "it is a gradual hardening process on both sides,—the
owner growing more and more cruel, as the servant more and more
callous." Ophelia retorts that the institution of slavery makes people
behave in this manner, and not Northern educational practices to
which she adheres.

Topsy does progress in learning new skills and displaying her
talents, but she also continues to misbehave. When Ophelia questions her as to why she still rebels, Topsy replies, "I spects cause I's
so wicked!" Topsy then encourages Ophelia to whip her because
as a "neglected, abused child," the girl is used to being beaten to
work and behave. Ophelia does so, but Topsy later brags to the other
slave children of her misdeeds and hardiness at taking punishment.

Analysis

In this chapter, Topsy provides St. Clare and Miss Ophelia with
a concrete example of slavery's ills. The St. Clare cousins, however,
reach different conclusions on the subject. St. Clare purchases
Topsy to prove the shortsightedness of Ophelia's indictments
against slavery. He challenges Ophelia, stating to her: "You're always preaching about educating." St. Clare foists Topsy on Ophelia,
knowing that the slave girl is misbehaved. He does so partly to mock
his cousin, and partly to save Topsy from her brutal masters. St.
Clare is "a mischievous fellow" who enjoys surprising and rattling
Ophelia. Yet he is also humane, pitying Topsy's mistreatment.

Ophelia is quite astonished when she is presented with Topsy.
As in the previous chapters, St. Clare chides Ophelia about her self-
righteous Northern attitude toward Southern slave owners, and
now points to her own reluctance to follow through on her prin-

ciples. Ophelia realizes that her cousin has trapped her in potential hypocrisy, and she must take in Topsy as her ward. When Topsy continually misbehaves, Ophelia resorts to whipping her, doing much the same thing she attacks slave holders for. St. Clare brings to mind the case of Prue, who had been whipped to death, indicating how this brutality can occur so often. He explains that punishment affects both slaves and masters, and that he would rather indulge his servants than to become harsh himself from disciplining too much.

St. Clare's and Miss Ophelia's views address the theme of individual vs. societal responsibility raised earlier. Ophelia argues that society as a whole must take initiative to right slavery's wrongs, but she avoids individual responsibility until St. Clare exposes this weakness in her discussion. St. Clare observes that societal pressure to uphold slavery is too strong to fight against, and he is powerless as an individual to oppose it.

Topsy herself baffles almost everyone in the household, except for St. Clare, who delights in her mischief. Because of her slave status, she repeats self-degrading statements made earlier by other slaves, following the theme of dehumanization. When Topsy says that she has never been born, she sounds like George Harris and Prue in their most distressing moments. When Ophelia asks her why she remains incorrigible, Topsy says that she is wicked. This comment is also made by Prue in her misery. Topsy does not understand anything outside of a brutalized life, and takes for granted that she is wicked. As Ophelia accuses St. Clare, "It is your system [that] makes such children," to which he agrees. Only later does Topsy begin to soften under the loving influence of Eva, as will be seen later.

Study Questions

1. What does Topsy do at St. Clare's request to show Miss Ophelia?

2. How does Ophelia protest the imposition of Topsy upon her?

3. How did St. Clare first learn about Topsy?

4. What does Ophelia see on Topsy when giving her a bath?

5. Why does Topsy not know who her parents are, or how old she is?

6. What does Ophelia first teach Topsy how to do?

7. Why does Topsy confess to stealing things that she did not take?

8. What does Eva command of the other servants regarding Topsy?

9. Why does Ophelia give in to whipping Topsy?

10. What does St. Clare disapprove of in Ophelia's education of Topsy?

Answers

1. She sings and dances.

2. She protests by saying that the whole house is already full of servants who need education, and Topsy would only add to her burden.

3. He first learned about Topsy when he passed by a restaurant in which she was screaming because of the beatings her masters gave her.

4. She sees welts and other spots on Topsy's back as a result of the whippings.

5. Topsy does not know any of her personal information because she was raised by slave traders from birth and received no education.

6. Ophelia first teaches her how to make a bed.

7. Topsy confesses to taking other things because she is afraid that Ophelia will beat her anyway.

8. Eva commands that no one may scorn Topsy.

9. Ophelia gives in to whipping Topsy because she ran out of other ideas on disciplining her ward.

10. He disapproves of Ophelia teaching Topsy the catechism and other religious topics.

Suggested Essay Topics

1. How does St. Clare try to get Ophelia to behave like a slave holder? Is he successful?

2. Discuss Topsy's background. How does she compare to the other St. Clare servants? To other slaves in the book?

Chapter 21

Summary

This chapter returns to the Shelby plantation. Aunt Chloe has received Uncle Tom's letter that St. Clare had written for him. Mrs. Shelby in the mean time brings up the subject to her husband of buying back Tom. Mr. Shelby, however, is still financially troubled and cannot spare the money for purchasing his former servant. When Mrs. Shelby offers to help with the debts, Mr. Shelby retorts: "You don't know anything about business." But as the author points out, Mrs. Shelby possessed "a clear, energetic, practical mind, and a force of character every way superior to that of her husband." She offers to give music lessons to raise money, but Mr. Shelby refuses to dishonor the family in this way by having his wife work.

Aunt Chloe proposes to hire herself out to a baker and earn the extra dollars needed to buy back her husband. Mrs. Shelby agrees to this arrangement and promises to contribute what she can too. The chapter closes with Master George planning to write back to Tom and reporting what will be done to reunite him with his family.

Analysis

Here Mr. and Mrs. Shelby once again delve into the practical and moral aspects of slavery. Mrs. Shelby addresses the theme of family, believing that Tom should be with his own kin, even though he is with a humane master, St. Clare. She declares to Mr. Shelby: "I have taught my people that their marriages are as sacred as ours." Mrs. Shelby includes Christian principles in her teachings, believing that slaves are humans with souls that require salvation.

Mr. Shelby responds that he lacks the funds to buy Tom, and that Tom will form other familial attachments under his new owner. Mr. Shelby also dismisses his wife's efforts at incorporating religion into the servants' lives. As he states: "It's a pity, wife, that you have burdened them with a morality above their condition and prospects." He thinks that his wife sets unrealistic educational and moral goals because she raises the slaves' expectations for a better life. Although a kind master himself, Mr. Shelby knows that slaves ultimately are considered property.

Mr. and Mrs. Shelby repeat their arguments presented in the beginning of the novel when the issue of selling Tom and Harry first arose. Mrs. Shelby constantly resorts to the humane and Christian argument that servants are part of the larger plantation family. Mr. Shelby maintains that the practical, business side of slavery must predominate his concerns. His wife, however, also has a good mind for business and offers her advice, which Mr. Shelby rejects out of pride. In effect, Mrs. Shelby counters her husband's arguments with both humanitarian and pragmatic reasons. In her sound and compassionate judgment, she allows Chloe to work for the extra money to re-purchase Tom.

Mr. and Mrs. Shelby's discussion resembles Senator and Mrs. Bird's, when they also debate the ethical and practical issues that arise from slavery. Like Mrs. Bird, Mrs. Shelby in this chapter repeats her hatred for slavery because of its immoral effects on the family.

Study Questions

1. When does Mrs. Shelby decide to talk to Mr. Shelby about buying Tom?

2. What is Mr. Shelby's initial reaction to hearing that Tom is being treated well?

3. What is Mrs. Shelby's first suggestion to her husband for raising money to buy Tom?

4. What is Mrs. Shelby's second suggestion after Mr. Shelby rejects her first?

5. In what roundabout way does Chloe bring up the subject of working for a baker to earn money?

6. Where is the baker located?

7. How did Chloe learn about working for the baker?

8. How much would Chloe earn from her work?

9. What does Chloe ask Mrs. Shelby about Louisville?

10. When does Chloe decide to go?

Answers

1. Mrs. Shelby decides to talk to her husband when he is smoking his after-dinner cigar.

2. Mr. Shelby initially is glad to hear that Tom is being treated well, but his mood changes when Mrs. Shelby wants to buy Tom.

3. She suggests that Mr. Shelby sell some of his horses and one of his farms.

4. She suggests that she could give music lessons.

5. Chloe first asks about how Mrs. Shelby would like the chicken cooked.

6. The baker is located in Louisville, Kentucky.

7. She learned about the baker from Sam.

8. Chloe would earn four dollars a week.

9. She asks Mrs. Shelby how far Louisville is from where Uncle Tom is. Chloe had hoped to be near enough to visit her husband, but Mrs. Shelby tells her that she would still be too far away to see Tom.

10. She decides to go the next day.

Suggested Essay Topics

1. Why is Mr. Shelby unwilling to buy back Tom? What does he disagree about with his wife?

2. Discuss the importance of family to Mrs. Shelby and Aunt Chloe. In what ways do they differ?

Chapters 22, 23, and 24

New Characters:

Alfred St. Clare: *Augustine St. Clare's twin brother*

Henrique: *Alfred's arrogant, twelve-year-old son*

Dodo: *Henrique's thirteen-year-old servant*

Summary

These chapters focus primarily on Eva and her influence on other characters. Two years pass, and Uncle Tom still looks forward to the day when he can return to his family on the Shelby plantation. When the summer arrives, the entire St. Clare household moves to a villa near Lake Pontchartrain in Louisiana. Tom and Eva have become even closer friends than before, and as they sit by the lake, Eva has a vision of heaven. She prophesies her own early death, pointing to the sky and declaring: "I'm going there...to the spirits bright." Sometime previously, both Tom and Miss Ophelia had noticed Eva's weakening condition. When Ophelia tries to tell St. Clare that his daughter is becoming seriously ill, he ignores her warnings out of the fear of losing Eva.

As Eva watches Topsy and the other slave children play, she inquires of her mother why they do not teach the servants to read. Marie St. Clare thinks that Eva asks peculiar questions, answering that servants were made to work and nothing else. Eva desires to set up a school in the North some day and teach blacks to read and write, as well as provide them with religious instruction. Marie only laughs at her daughter's dreams.

Augustine's twin brother, Alfred, along with his son, Henrique, join the St. Clare group at the summer villa. Henrique, a "noble, dark-eyed, princely boy, full of vivacity and spirit," plans to go riding with Eva. When Dodo, his servant, brings out Henrique's horse, the St. Clare boy chastises him for not brushing the animal. Dodo attempts to explain that the horse had gotten itself dirty shortly after being cleaned, but Henrique becomes enraged and strikes him. Uncle Tom verifies Dodo's story, and Eva cautions Henrique: "You frighten him into deceiving, if you treat him so." Henrique tosses

his servant a coin to quash his own guilt, but Eva kindly talks to Dodo, treating him as a human being. Eva then makes Henrique promise her that he will act more humanely toward Dodo, telling her cousin to even love his servant.

Augustine and Alfred St. Clare observe the incident and discuss Henrique's character. Augustine wryly notes that Henrique is a natural aristocrat who considers his fellow humans with contempt. Alfred realizes his son's temperament, but defends Henrique's actions, stating: "It is the educated, the intelligent, the wealthy, the refined, who ought to have equal rights." The "greasy masses," he continues, deserve no such rights. Augustine responds by pointing to the examples of the American and French Revolutions, from which the rhetoric of liberty and equality had emerged.

After Alfred and Henrique depart, Eva's health worsens. Marie begins to show some maternal concern for her daughter, but only when Miss Ophelia brings Eva's condition to her attention. Eva later tells Tom that she would gladly die for the happiness of the servants, knowing how they suffer. She also makes St. Clare promise to free Tom after she dies.

Analysis

In each of these three chapters, Eva asserts her loving, spiritual influence on several of the characters. The author states that Eva's "whole heart and soul seemed absorbed in works of love and kindness." Because of Uncle Tom's feelings for her, his exile from his family is less miserable for him. When Eva foreshadows her own death as she views the light reflected off the lake's surface, Tom never doubts her. He "loved her as something frail and earthly, yet almost worshipped her as something heavenly and divine."

St. Clare preoccupies himself more with material than spiritual concerns and denies Eva's decline in health. Since Eva is the one person whom he adores the most, he cannot absorb the fact that she is dying. Eva tells him that she is going to heaven, and St. Clare thinks back to his own boyhood when his own mother sang religious hymns. He tries to remember the past spiritual life that he had once experienced. When Eva asks why so much suffering exists, especially for slaves, St. Clare cannot answer specifically. Eva then desires that Tom be freed since she knows that if anything happened to her father, the servants' future would be dangerously uncertain.

Eva displays her willingness to help slaves when she asks her mother why they are denied an education, recalling the theme of slaves as property vs. as humans. Marie St. Clare cannot move beyond her own selfish thoughts, laughing at her daughter's saintly desires for the servants, whom Marie considers as nothing more than property. But because Eva thinks of the servants as humans with souls, she wishes that they could be taught to read, and specifically the Bible. When Eva becomes increasingly sick, Marie starts to worry, but with the view that her dying daughter only added to her own misery.

Eva affects her cousin Henrique for the better when she confronts his mistreatment of Dodo. Because Henrique is used to a life of command and his own sense of superiority, he cannot stand attempts at insubordination. He beats Dodo thinking that the servant is trying to hide his own carelessness. Eva pleas with her cousin to be more humane, telling him, "dear Cousin, do love poor Dodo, and be kind to him, for my sake!" Henrique promises to follow her wishes because of his own respect and admiration for Eva.

Augustine and Alfred St. Clare discuss the wider significance of Henrique's character and the effects of slavery on it. Augustine touches on the theme of dehumanization, observing to his brother about young masters: "Our system is educating them in barbarism and brutality. We are breaking all humanizing ties." He argues that slavery adversely affects slave owners as well as their servants. Alfred is aware of Henrique's passionate character, but only responds that the system "makes boys manly and courageous." Augustine presses the issue by noting that oppression has its limits on those it affects the most, namely the oppressed. He points to revolutions occurring throughout the world. When Alfred states that only whites are capable of forming revolutions, Augustine counters that many slaves have white parents, specifically masters who had taken advantage of their slaves.

The theme of the Christ-like character reappears in Chapter 22 and 24, but in Eva this time rather than Tom. Much like Christ, she foreshadows her own death and expresses her desire to give up her own life for the sake of the servants. As Tom explains to

Mammy regarding Eva, "She's got the Lord's mark in her forehead."
He states this metaphorically, meaning that Eva appears chosen
by God to die for the good of others.

Study Questions

1. How does Uncle Tom hear about his family on the Shelby
    plantation?

2. What prompts Eva to think about heaven as she and Tom sit
    by the lake?

3. Whom does Eva decide to teach how to read after her mother
    scoffs at the idea?

4. Why does Henrique strike Dodo?

5. What saying does Augustine St. Clare quote to his brother
    regarding the dangers of Henrique's loss of self-control?

6. What does St. Clare worry about after Eva and Henrique re-
    turn from their ride?

7. Who first brings Eva's state of health to the attention of Au-
    gustine and Marie St. Clare?

8. What does Eva wish to her father regarding the servants?

9. What sufferings does Eva refer to when talking about the
    servants?

10. What does St. Clare promise to do for Eva after she dies?

Answers

1. He hears about his family from a letter he received from
    young Master George, who had written for Aunt Chloe.

2. She reads a Bible passage, "And I saw a sea of glass, mingled
    with fire," that prompts her thoughts on heaven.

3. Eva decides to teach Mammy how to read.

4. He strikes Dodo because Henrique's horse has dirt on it, and
    Henrique thinks that Dodo failed to clean it properly.

5. Augustine quotes, "They that cannot govern themselves can-
    not govern others."

6. He worries about his daughter's health, seeing that she is fatigued by the ride.

7. Miss Ophelia brings the news of Eva's declining health to her parents, but neither Augustine nor Marie are initially willing to believe it.

8. She wishes that the servants were all free.

9. She talks about how Prue's and Mammy's children had been taken from them.

10. He promises to free Tom.

Suggested Essay Topics

1. Compare and contrast the spiritual nature of Eva and Tom.

2. Discuss Eva's role in the confrontation between Henrique and Dodo. What does she say to each?

3. Compare and contrast Augustine and Alfred St. Clare's opinions on the ruling class.

Chapters 25, 26, and 27

Summary

These chapters continue with a focus on Eva and her influence on the St. Clare household, especially on Topsy. In Chapter 25, Miss Ophelia discovers that one of her bonnets has been destroyed by Topsy. When St. Clare questions Topsy about her mischief, she answers: "Spects it's my wicked heart." Ophelia decides that she can no longer tolerate Topsy's antics and wants to give up on her. St. Clare forces Ophelia to reconsider, however, when he again raises the issue of her supposed Christian endurance.

Eva draws Topsy aside to find out why the servant girl misbehaves. Topsy repeats her history of having no family and no one to love her. She also knows that Ophelia personally dislikes her, saying: "No; she can't bar me, 'cause I'm a nigger!—she'd soon have a toad touch her!" Eva declares that she loves Topsy and encourages her to be good for Eva's sake. Eva then tells Topsy about Christ's love for everyone.

In Chapter 26, Eva weakens more and is confined to her bedroom. Topsy brings her flowers, although she is first stopped from doing so by Marie St. Clare. Eva explains to her mother that Topsy is trying to behave and overcome her brutal past. Eva then requests that some of her own hair be cut so that she can distribute the locks to everyone. Calling the whole household into her room, Eva dispenses her locks and reminds everbody of their Christian duties. After most have left, Eva asks her father if he believes in the Christian faith. Despite his own humanity toward others, St. Clare replies that he is unsure of his own salvation. Eva then passes away amid her grieving family.

In Chapter 27, Topsy mourns over Eva's death, crying "O, Miss Eva!...I wish I's dead, too." Her grief is particularly great. With Eva's passing, Topsy feels that no one will love her. Moved herself by Eva's death, Miss Ophelia reassures Topsy: "I can love you; I do, and I'll try to help you to grow up a good Christian girl."

After the household returns from Lake Pontchartrain to New Orleans, St. Clare questions Uncle Tom about his faith. St. Clare admits that he still has trouble believing in Christianity. Tom responds that he feels the Lord in his soul and prays for his master.

Analysis

When Ophelia is at her wits' end regarding Topsy, Eva once again intervenes with her Christian love and patience. She transforms how both Topsy and Ophelia feel toward one another. As in Chapter 23, when Eva advises her cousin Henrique to love and care for his servant Dodo, here she pleads with Topsy to behave. Topsy realizes what Ophelia thinks of her, and Ophelia even admits: "I've always had a prejudice against negroes...and it's a fact, I never could bear to have that child touch me." When Eva expresses her love for Topsy, the servant girl who had known nothing but hatred and brutality accepts that love.

The theme of the Christ-like figure appears when St. Clare jokingly upbraids his cousin for her impatience and unchristian attitude toward Topsy. Ophelia points to Eva's self-sacrificing, devout character, referring to St. Clare's daughter as "no more than Christlike." Through this statement, Ophelia in a way realizes her own shortcomings as a Christian by admitting to Eva's perfect Christian love for people no matter how they have sinned. But Eva's example prods Ophelia to become more loving toward Topsy, fulfilling Christ's yearning for his followers to show unconditional love for one another.

When Eva nears death, she shares some final thoughts with everyone. By urging her family and servants to keep leading Christian lives, she wishes that they would continue to care for one another according to Christ's bidding. The ornaments in Eva's bedroom contribute to the imagery of her own divine character. Sculptured angels and a statuette of Christ with little children adorn her bed and fireplace mantle. Although Topsy has been trying to behave, the other servants and family members rebuke her, being used to her mischief. Eva, however, is more patient and invites her into the room to receive flowers that Topsy had brought. Eva is aware of Topsy's efforts to display affection. When Marie St. Clare expresses her doubts regarding Topsy's sincerity, Eva explains the circumstances of Topsy's upbringing and compares it to her own. Eva justifies her own goodness through the friends and family that offer her love and comfort. Topsy, on the other hand, had known no family or friend, but only brutal slave traders. Eva's comparison repeats the theme that slavery is dehumanizing, making a person like Topsy into a devious and tough child.

Topsy feels the loss of Eva the most. She repeats the statement that other slaves in their misery have said, bemoaning in dialect: "I jist wish I hadn't never been born." A sense of redemption occurs, however, when Ophelia decides not to give up on her ward. Since Eva's death, Ophelia declares that she will love Topsy, attributing her own changed attitude to Eva's influence.

Marie St. Clare still remains her same pouting self. Her husband is too grief-stricken to even cry over their daughter's death, and Marie mistakes this lack of emotional display as St. Clare's unconcern for Eva. St. Clare turns to Tom for comfort, seeking spiritual relief for his earthly anguish. Tom's faith, however, cannot penetrate St. Clare's worldview. The situation is tragic for both characters. Tom grieves for St. Clare's unbelief, and St. Clare himself desires to have faith, but cannot or will not because of his sense of material reality.

Study Questions

1. Where was Miss Ophelia when Topsy cut up the bonnet?

2. What does Marie St. Clare advise that Ophelia should do with Topsy?

3. What does Eva's lecture to Topsy remind St. Clare of?

4. What reasoning does Eva give to try to convince her mother of Topsy's goodness?

5. Why does Eva give everyone a lock of her hair?

6. What service does Uncle Tom perform for Eva during her last days?

7. After Eva dies, what does Topsy still want to bring into the bedroom?

8. When St. Clare does not weep at his daughter's death, what does Marie think?

9. When St. Clare reads Eva's Bible, what does he confess to Tom?

10. What does St. Clare request of Tom?

Answers

1. Miss Ophelia had gone to a Methodist meeting with Eva.

2. She advises Ophelia to whip Topsy.

3. Eva reminds St. Clare of his own mother.

4. Eva tells her mother that God had made everyone, and therefore everyone had a soul that required nurturing.

5. Eva gives everyone a lock of her hair so that they are reminded that she loves them and will see them in heaven.

6. Tom carries Eva around the house and gardens.

7. Topsy still wants to bring in flowers.

8. Marie mistakenly thinks that St. Clare had no sympathy for Eva.

9. He confesses to Tom that he still cannot believe in religion.

10. He requests that Tom pray for him.

Suggested Essay Topics

1. Discuss Eva's effect on the spiritual life of Topsy. Why do others fail to influence Topsy?

2. Examine St. Clare's attitude toward religion. How are his views affected by Eva's death?

3. What is Uncle Tom's role during these trying moments? How does he counsel St. Clare?

Chapters 28 and 29

Summary

After returning from the lake villa to the New Orleans mansion, St. Clare tries to make sense of Eva's death. Although refraining from spiritual considerations, he reads Eva's Bible and thinks more seriously about his role as slave holder. St. Clare then decides to free Tom.

Miss Ophelia also changes in character, becoming more lenient and understanding toward Topsy. Ophelia approaches St. Clare to have him make out papers of Topsy's ownership to her so that she can bring Topsy north to freedom. St. Clare jokes with Ophelia at this suggestion, asking her: "What will the Abolition Society think...if you become a slave-holder!" Ophelia, however, is well-intentioned toward Topsy's future and well aware of the "fiction of law" that made Topsy a piece of property. Ophelia also brings up the future of St. Clare's other servants in case something should happen to their master, but St. Clare shrugs off his cousin's concern.

St. Clare moves to a discussion with Ophelia regarding emancipation, or freeing the slaves. He announces that he is now willing to emancipate his servants. "I am braver that I was," he says, "because I have lost all." But St. Clare remains skeptical about the future of freed slaves because of many whites' reluctance to educate or socialize with blacks. As he asks his cousin, "If we emancipate, will you educate?" Ophelia replies that she is ready and willing.

Later in the evening, St. Clare goes out for a stroll. Soon afterwards, however, he is brought back into the house, mortally wounded. Several people explain that St. Clare had come across a

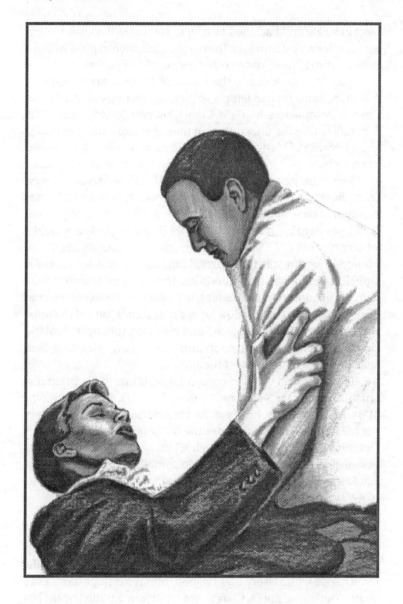

fight at a cafe and had tried to stop it. He received a knife wound for his efforts. St. Clare asks Tom to pray, but then expires without having written Tom's or the other servants' free papers.

After St. Clare's death, the future of his servants comes into question. Since he had left no written instructions as to what he desired for the slaves, Marie St. Clare takes possession of them. The servants realize the uncertainty of their situation, and it frightens them because of Marie's supportive views on slavery. St. Clare had been an indulgent master, but such is not the case with his wife.

Two situations occur that only confirm the servants' worst fears. Rosa, one of Marie's personal servants, is ordered by her mistress to be whipped for talking back to Marie. Rosa appeals to Miss Ophelia to intervene. Ophelia does so, but is rebuked by Marie, who says of Rosa, "I'll give her one lesson that will bring her down, I fancy!" The threat is then carried out. Later Uncle Tom asks for Ophelia's help when he reminds her that St. Clare had promised Tom his freedom. Ophelia agrees, but again her pleas are rejected by Marie. The St. Clare widow knows that Tom is "one of the most valuable servants on the place," and seeks to profit by him. Marie shows no concern for the servants' well-being, standing firm against emancipating any of them.

Tom's reaction to his uncertain future is one of Christian resignation, as he says: "The Lord's will be done!" Despite his attempt at spiritual assurance, however, Tom is saddened that he may never see his family again, and shares the other servants' worries. Miss Ophelia writes a letter to Mrs. Shelby, letting her know about Tom's circumstances and urging her to do something for him. Chapter 29 closes with a slave trader taking Tom and some other servants to a slave warehouse to be sold at an auction.

Analysis

In Chapter 28, St. Clare's tragic life comes to an end. Previously, he had experienced other misfortunes: marriage to a selfish wife, his struggle with slavery and religion, and most important, Eva's death. The tragedy of St. Clare's own death is magnified by his latest intention and decision to free his slaves. Because of Ophelia's personal concern and foresight, she makes sure that Topsy will not spend her life as a slave any longer. Due to St. Clare's own carelessness, he delays making out papers for his other servants, including Tom. With his untimely murder, St. Clare leaves them unprotected in any legal manner.

St. Clare foreshadows his own death when he earlier thinks about his mother, who had raised him religiously and had long since died. Before he walks to the cafe where the scuffle occurs, St. Clare eerily says, "I don't know what makes me think of my mother so much, to-night." On his deathbed, St. Clare's last word is "Mother!"

In Chapter 29, the ramifications of St. Clare's tragic death becomes clearer for his slaves. Without legal protection, the servants are still regarded as property, and along with the rest of the estate, may be kept or sold depending on Marie's whims. In fact, Marie decides to sell the mansion, along with all the servants, and return to her father's plantation. Her own selfishness becomes apparent when Miss Ophelia tries to appeal her decisions about the slaves. Marie, however, responds: "Everybody is against me!...Everybody is so inconsiderate!" She believes that because she lost Eva and then St. Clare, her sufferings are the greatest, even though she had only cared for herself when they were alive.

Miss Ophelia displays her humanity when attempting to intervene on the servants' behalf. Especially with Tom, she feels moved to confront Marie regarding his future. Since Marie had thought all along that slaves are more content in servility than with their own freedom, the reader is not surprised by her response to sell Tom. "Keep a negro under the care of a master," Marie concludes, "and he does well enough." Miss Ophelia, with the "strong New England blood of liberty" in her veins, is outraged by Marie's opinions, reminding the widow of her late husband's last wishes. Because Ophelia's attempts are futile, she decides that the only recourse is for Mrs. Shelby to hurry with her intentions of buying Tom back.

The author uses irony and sarcasm to depict Marie St. Clare's character. Although a heartless and self-centered woman, Marie perceives herself as a victim preyed upon by Miss Ophelia and the servants. Marie thinks that the servants are spoiled, mainly because of her husband's kindly and overindulgent nature. She believes that Ophelia is the one who is inconsiderate because Ophelia supposedly disrespects Marie's state of mourning with the servants' concerns.

Stowe uses the theme of legal protection to show the uncertainties connected with a slave status. As she explains: "The child who has lost a father has still the protection of friends, and of the law." The slave, on the other hand, receives protection "through the sovereign and irresponsible will of his master." When the master dies, "nothing remains" for the slave except uncertainty.

The theme of breaking up families continues in these chapters. Adolph, Rosa, and other personal servants within the St. Clare household had been together for a long time. With the breakup of the estate, they will be separated from each other and the home that they have known. Tom, who previously had hoped to rejoin his family in Kentucky, now faces the obstacle of being further moved from it.

Study Questions

1. Why does St. Clare feel that with Eva's death, he has lost everything?

2. Why does St. Clare keep company with Tom more and more?

3. Before his plans to return to Kentucky, what does Tom promise to do for St. Clare?

4. Why does Miss Ophelia want to legally own Topsy?

5. What is St. Clare's concern once the servants are emancipated?

6. Why are the servants worried about their future?

7. What does Marie intend to prove by sending Rosa to the whipping-house?

8. How does Tom hear about the servants being sold?

9. How does Miss Ophelia invoke Eva's and St. Clare's names to argue for Tom's freedom?

10. What does Miss Ophelia hope to accomplish by writing to Mrs. Shelby?

Answers

1. St. Clare feels that he has lost everything that was important to him because he had done everything for Eva's sake. Now that she is dead, St. Clare senses a loss in purpose.

2. He keeps company with Tom because the pious servant reminds St. Clare of Eva's spirituality and innocence.

3. Tom promises that he will stay with St. Clare until St. Clare's soul is no longer troubled.

4. She wants to legally own Topsy to free her when they go north.

5. His concern is that once the servants are free, they will travel north for jobs and face stiff prejudice from Northerners.

6. They are worried because they know Marie is not as kind as St. Clare had been to them, and they think she will sell them.

7. Marie intends on shaming Rosa, whom she feels has too much haughtiness anyway.

8. Tom hears the news from Adolph, who had overheard Marie's conversation with a lawyer.

9. She invokes their names by mentioning to Marie that their last wishes concerned Tom's freedom.

10. She hopes that Mrs. Shelby, once knowing Tom's situation, would send someone to buy Tom.

Suggested Essay Topics

1. How does Eva's death affect St. Clare's views on religion?

2. Discuss Marie St. Clare's behavior regarding setting Tom free. How does it coincide with her views on slavery? Why does she think that no one cares for her own concerns?

3. Compare Tom's reaction to being sold to Adolph's. Why is Tom more calm and accepting of the circumstances?

Chapters 30, 31, and 32

New Characters:

Mr. Skeggs: *keeper of a slave warehouse*

Sambo: *slave in Skeggs's warehouse*

Susan and Emmeline: *mother and daughter auctioned off separately*

Simon Legree: *brutal master who buys Tom and Emmeline*

Sambo and Quimbo: *Legree's drivers, slaves themselves*

Lucy: *slave whom Legree purchased for Sambo*

Summary

Chapter 30 depicts the slave warehouse owned by Mr. Skeggs, at which Tom and the other St. Clare servants arrive. The slaves are kept "well fed, well cleaned, tended, and looked after" to bring the highest prices from bidders at the upcoming auction. Sambo, a large and tough slave whom Mr. Skeggs keeps to entertain the other slaves, immediately greets and mocks the new arrivals. Mr. Skeggs wants the slaves to appear merry and contented, forcing them to sing and dance, despite their sorrowful moods.

In the women's warehouse, a slave mother and her daughter, Susan and Emmeline, are introduced here. They discuss the possibilities of their being sold together; Emmeline is young and hopeful while her mother frets about being separated. Both have been raised in a religious home by a kind woman. The owner's son, however, had been careless in managing the estate and consequently fell into debt. Susan and Emmeline therefore had to be sold.

Simon Legree first appears in this chapter, at whom Tom "felt an immediate and revolting horror…, that increased as he came near." Legree possesses a "round, bullet head," a "large, coarse mouth," and hands that are "immensely large, hairy, sun-burned, freckled, and very dirty." He forcefully inspects Tom and Emmeline, eventually buying them at the auction. A humane gentleman purchases Susan, and at her pleas, tries to bid for Emmeline as well to keep them together. Legree, however, is intent on getting Emmeline and outbids everyone for her.

After purchasing his slaves, Legree puts them on a boat and heads for his plantation on the Red River in Louisiana. He barters off Tom's clothes and trunk to the boat crew, but Tom manages to hide his Bible from Legree. Legree then tells his newly purchased servants that he shows no mercy and is used to beating his slaves, displaying for them his huge, ironlike fist. Two gentlemen, one a Southerner and the other a Northerner, overhear Legree's speech. The Southerner apologetically comments that Legree cannot be taken as an example of how masters treat their slaves. The Northerner, however, criticizes his companion, noting that respectable Southern gentlemen play an important part in supporting the system that gives rise to such men as Legree.

Meanwhile Emmeline meets Lucy, one of the other slaves bought by Legree. Emmeline learns that Lucy had been separated from her husband and four children. Both Emmeline and Lucy have been raised religiously, but have difficulty finding comfort in their faith because they are terrified by Legree.

Upon arriving at Legree's "desolate and uncomfortable" plantation, the group is greeted by Sambo and Quimbo, two slaves who are Legree's drivers, or overseers. Legree has cruelly manipulated them into hating one another, and setting them against the rest of the fieldhands. Lucy is given to Sambo as a new mate, Emmeline goes unwillingly with Legree, and the remaining slaves, including Tom, are shown their rundown lodgings.

Later in the evening, Legree's fieldhands return to their cabins. Tom helps two women who are too tired to cook their own dinner. Touched by his kindness, they chat with him, and Tom tells them about the Bible. As Tom falls asleep afterwards, he dreams of little Eva, which consoles him somewhat.

Analysis

Chapter 30 presents various aspects of the slave trade, examining how several different parties are involved. The reader is first introduced to Mr. Skeggs, who tries to make the slaves as presentable as possible. He is mainly concerned with turning a profit and knows that he must force a certain amount of happiness on them through the antics of Sambo. The author here relates how a New York law firm is in charge of handling the debts and credits of slave holders. Northerners, Stowe emphasizes, are involved in the slave trade as well.

The theme of breaking up families again emerges in this chapter. Describing the auction, Stowe lists family members up for sale, rather than just servants. The reader, she notes, "shall find an abundance of husbands, wives, brothers, sisters, fathers, mothers, and young children" to be sold. She uses sarcasm when portraying the skills of the slave traders in selling their wares because they have "learned the art of sinning expertly and genteelly."

The separation of mother and daughter is personified by Susan and Emmeline. The mother constantly worries, and with good reason, that they will be separated at the auction. They both try to live according to Christian principles that had been taught by their mistress. This chapter repeats the previous theme of slaves as humans or property. Stowe addresses the reader directly, asking how anyone would feel if they were about to be bought without knowing their future owner. She emphasizes the inhumanity of slavery, writing that they "can be sold, leased, mortgaged, exchanged for groceries or dry goods, to suit the phases of trade, or the fancy of the purchaser." The irony of the situation resembles Mrs. Shelby's instruction of her servants earlier in the book. The well-intentioned owners try to imbue their servants with moral standards by which to live, but cannot stop the inhumane sales that eventually tear the slave families apart.

Chapters 31 and 32 provide a more indepth look at Simon Legree's character and his effect on the servants. The reader has no doubt that Legree is a barbaric man. He brags to other boat passengers that he buys and works slaves to death, keeping continuously to this cycle, rather than spending time and money caring for them. He also chides the more humane slave owners, boasting in dialect, "I'm none o' yer gentlemen planters, with lily fingers." Legree prides himself on having a big, tough fist with which to knock down slaves. Tom's fears of getting a hard master are essentially realized when he becomes Legree's property.

Taking most of Tom's possessions, Legree discovers that Tom is religious, but mocks him, declaring "I'm your church now!" Tom has no response other than an inward, spiritual defiance in which he remembers and recites scriptural passages to himself. This con-

flict between Legree and Tom, the impious and the saintly, will
become more apparent as the book continues. The theme of Tom
as a Christ-figure reappears when Legree sells Tom's clothes to the
boat hands. This incident foreshadows Tom's future, which can be
compared to that of Christ's when Roman soldiers rolled dice for
his robe at the Crucifixion.

The discussion between the Northern and Southern gentlemen reflects the author's critique of slavery on a wider institutional
level, and not just of individuals. The Southerner apologizes for
Legree's crudeness, indicting him personally for his own faults of
brutality. The Northerner points to the larger issues of systematic
support that slavery has received to survive in the South. He notes
that if the Legrees were the only ones who abused slavery, it would
not last. But because gentlemen directly and indirectly protect and
defend slavery, they are as much to blame as Legree.

The author's description of Legree's plantation characterizes
the gloom of its inhabitants. A "wild, forsaken road" leads up to
the place, with its "dreary pine barrens," "doeful trees," and "fune-
real black moss." The newly acquired slaves themselves have a
"sunken and dejected expression." Legree plans to make Emmeline
his mistress, but she is horrified by her master. Sambo and Quimbo
have been dehumanized, operating on hate and distrust. The other
fieldhands are "surly and uncomfortable." Lucy is taken by Sambo,
only for her to respond in dialect, "Wish't I was dead!" Her misery
in slavery is such that, like other slaves in the book, would prefer
death than life in servitude.

Tom is the only figure who provides some hope and comfort
to others with his spiritual assurance. When he aids the two women,
they are grateful, not being used to kind deeds on Legree's plantation. Tom tells them about Christian love, but his listeners fail to
believe that a faith like his could survive in their hell.

Study Questions

1. What does Tom bring with him to the slave warehouse?

2. Why are some of the bidders unwilling to buy St. Clare's servants?

3. What last words of advice does Susan give to Emmeline?

4. What does Simon Legree want to know about Tom before the auction?

5. When Susan is bought by a humane gentleman, what does he try to do at her request?

6. When Simon Legree searches through Tom's possessions, what does he find that tells him that Tom is religious?

7. What plans does Legree have for Tom and Emmeline?

8. Why does Legree frequently purchase slaves?

9. Why is Legree's plantation run-down?

10. Describe Sambo and Quimbo.

Answers

1. He brings with him a trunk full of clothes.

2. Some bidders are unwilling to buy St. Clare's servants because they are thought to be too indulged and lazy.

3. In case they are separated, Susan tells her daughter to remember her Christian upbringing.

4. Legree questions Tom about where he was raised and what chores he did.

5. He tries to bid for Susan's daughter, Emmeline, but ultimately loses to Simon Legree.

6. Legree finds a Methodist hymn book among Tom's possessions.

7. He plans on using Tom to manage the plantation. Legree also wants to make Emmeline his mistress.

8. He finds buying slaves frequently is cheaper than actually taking care of them for long-term use.

9. Legree's plantation is rundown because he is too busy making money to take care of his place.

10. Sambo and Quimbo are vicious slaves who help Legree run the plantation. Legree has fostered a distrust and hatred between the two, so that they could tell on each other or on

the fieldhands. By this method, Legree would be aware of what happens on his plantation.

Suggested Essay Topics

1. Describe Susan's and Emmeline's relationship to one another. How is their background similar to Tom's?

2. What are Tom's and Emmeline's first impressions of Legree and his plantation?

3. Describe Legree's philosophy on managing his slaves and his plantation. How does his system differ from St. Clare's?

Chapters 33 and 34

New Character:

Cassy: *Simon Legree's defiant slave mistress*

Summary

As time passes, Tom still works diligently on the Legree plantation. Simon Legree thinks of making Tom into an overseer because of the slave's intelligence and hard work. But Legree is ultimately dissatisfied with Tom's upright character and seeks to make him more hardhearted like Sambo and Quimbo.

While Tom is working in the cotton fields, Cassy, Legree's slave mistress, labors next to him. Lucy also picks cotton, but is slower than the rest; Tom tries to help her by putting some of his cotton into her bag. Sambo sees this act and hits them both with his whip. Tom continues his aid despite Lucy's protest. Cassy then draws nearer to Tom, placing some of her own cotton into his bag, but warning him that the Legree plantation is too harsh for Tom to act kindly toward anyone.

When Sambo tells Legree of Tom's actions in the fields, Legree decides that he must break Tom of his charitable habits. After pretending that Lucy did not make her weight in cotton-picking, Legree commands Tom to whip her. Tom refuses, even though Legree confesses that he wants to promote Tom. Greatly angered by this stubborn refusal, Legree beats Tom savagely and then orders his two slave drivers to batter him more.

Tom is put in a shed to recuperate, and Cassy visits to nurse him. She tells him some of the brutal past on the Legree plantation, concluding: "There's no law here, of God or man, that can do you, or any one of us, the least good." Cassy then remarks that slaves cannot be individually accountable for their sins because of their terrible situation. Tom, however, replies that even though they can blame their difficult circumstances, "that won't keep us from growing wicked." He fears that he or anyone else would become as depraved as Sambo and Quimbo. Tom declares that he would rather die than be one of Legree's followers.

Cassy recounts her tormented past to Tom, telling him how she had received a Christian upbringing and how her father, a slave owner, had died before emancipating her. From then on, she was bought by and sold to several owners. She gave birth to several children who were sold from her, and eventually she ended up on Legree's plantation. Despite Tom's encouragement, Cassy cannot find the faith of her childhood religion anymore.

Analysis

The physical and spiritual struggle between Tom and Legree continues, and with harsh results for Tom. These chapters depict the tense and brutal situations that slaves must face. Tom is repeatedly beaten, a practice that he is unfamiliar with because of his previous kind masters, Mr. Shelby and St. Clare. Legree intends on making Tom one of the drivers and wants to toughen the slave's character. But Legree angrily discovers that the task will be difficult because of Tom's strong faith and refusal to participate in Legree's sins.

Tom's kindness becomes evident to others on the plantation when he helps Lucy with her load of cotton. At this point, the reader is introduced to Cassy, a thirty-five-year-old woman who has a mysterious connection to Legree. She has a character that appears "to convey...an idea of a wild, painful, and romantic history." Cassy aids Tom with his own cotton load, but with a warning that kindness provokes only trouble on Legree's place. "The Lord never visits these parts," she irreligiously states. Tom is whipped by Sambo,

but the driver stops short of hitting Cassy. This incident emphasizes Cassy's power to resist punishment. Something about her
character brings forth Sambo's respect and fear.

When Legree hears about Tom's benevolent deeds, he is more
determined to break the slave. Here again, the reader senses
Cassy's defiance and toughness. She speaks to Legree in French,
which is not deciphered by the others, but the effect of her words
angers Legree. He does not, however, strike her. Instead, he con-
trives to have Tom whip Lucy. Tom remains passively defiant by
calmly explaining that he will perform no such cruel acts against
anyone. Tom provides an example of the theme of nonviolent
resistence.

Legree at first had interpreted Tom's character as humble and
therefore easily broken. Tom, however, replies in dialect: "my soul
an't yours, Mas'r! You haven't bought it,—ye can't buy it!" Tom's response confuses and then vexes Legree to the extent that he and
his drivers beat the pious slave. Legree is used to exerting his power
and authority over others through material wealth and sheer physical force. He feels inadequate to answer Tom on a higher spiritual
plane, therefore, resorting to violence to conceal his moral inferi-
ority to his own servant.

In Chapter 34, the reader learns more about Cassy, who exem-
plifies the theme of slavery's dehumanization. After Tom is beaten
and taken to a shed, she visits and comforts him. Tom feels both
physical and spiritual pain, calling on God to help him. Cassy comments adversely on religion, drawing on a bitterness developed
over a long period on the plantation. She tells Tom some of her
past, in which she ended up as Legree's slave mistress. Cassy's
mother was a slave and her father a master. Through an incident
similar to Tom's, Cassy gets sold because her father, like St. Clare,
dies before he can emancipate her. She becomes the lover and
property of several masters, one of whom sells her children from
her. Cassy confesses that she had been religious when she was a
girl, but now only her bitterness and anger prevail as a result of
seeing her family broken up and living a hard life.

Study Questions

1. Why does Legree want to break Tom's gentle character?

2. What does Tom notice about Lucy that makes him help her in the fields?

3. When Sambo catches Tom helping Lucy, what is Legree's reaction when he learns about it?

4. What does Tom declare that he would rather do than whip somebody?

5. How does Legree try to argue his case on religious grounds for Tom to obey him?

6. When Legree says that he has purchased Tom body and soul, what is Tom's reply?

7. What does Cassy suggest that Tom give up after his beating?

8. How long has Cassy been on the Legree plantation?

9. From where is Cassy originally?

10. What happened to Cassy's last child when the others were sold from her?

Answers

1. Legree wants to break Tom and make him into an overseer. But to be effective to Legree, Tom must be brutal to get the most work out of the other slaves.

2. He notices that she is getting exhausted.

3. He tells Sambo and Quimbo that they all will have to break Tom.

4. Tom declares that he would rather die first than whip slaves.

5. He argues that the Bible says for servants to obey their masters.

6. Tom replies that Legree does not own the servant's soul, but God does.

7. She suggests that he give up being nice to people because Legree is too powerful.

8. She has been on the plantation for five years.

9. She is originally from New Orleans.

10. Cassy killed her last child so that it would not suffer a life in slavery.

Suggested Essay Topics

1. Compare Tom's and Legree's attitudes toward the management of slaves.

2. Describe Cassy's interaction with Legree and Sambo. What do her actions and attitudes tell about her character?

Chapters 35 and 36

Summary

In Chapter 35, Cassy confronts Legree about Tom's beating. She calls Legree's attention to his wastefulness of harming a good slave, especially at the height of the picking season. Earlier, he had threatened to put Cassy to work in the fields, which she actually did to show him the emptiness of his threats. Cassy knows that Legree keeps his distance from her. As she says to him: "You're afraid of me, Simon...and you've reason to be! But be careful, for I've got the devil in me!"

Sambo brings to Legree some of Tom's possessions: the dollar coin that Master George had given him, and Eva's lock of hair. Legree throws a fit of alarm at the sight of Eva's curls, throwing them into the fire and tossing the coin out the window. Here the reader learns about Legree's past, which further explains his behavior. He had been raised in New England by a devout mother. His father, however, was a coarse man, and Simon followed his rough habits. Going out to sea, Simon learns of his mother's death in a letter that contained a lock of her hair. This lock appears identical to Eva's and thus reminds Legree of his guilty conscience for spurning his mother and a moral life.

Legree vows to leave Tom alone after this episode, but remains scared by it. He invites Sambo and Quimbo into his house to help ward off his loneliness, and they all participate in a drunken revelry.

In Chapter 36, Cassy visits Emmeline. Emmeline declares that she would rather hide in the swamps surrounding the plantation than live any longer with Legree. Cassy, however, dissuades her, knowing that Legree would send out dogs after her. Cassy even recounts other past incidents in which Legree tortured his slaves once he had caught them. Cassy then advises Emmeline to get accustomed to life on the plantation, since it will not get any better.

Meanwhile, Legree tries to sleep off his drunkenness. He dreams of hearing faint voices and sees a veiled figure approaching him, which turns out to be his mother. Laughing, Cassy appears behind Legree, and she pushes him. Legree has a sensation of falling and then wakes in a horror-stricken panic.

The next morning, Cassy again confronts Legree regarding his ill treatment of Tom. She warns Legree that Tom will not break under any trying circumstance. Cassy repeats her reason for leaving Tom alone, stating that he is a good worker. Legree grudgingly concurs, but he still must have the last word, visiting Tom at the shed. Legree asks if Tom is ready to beg forgiveness. Tom reiterates his commitment to be a good laborer, but will not participate in any cruelty toward anyone. Legree once again becomes enraged and beats Tom. Cassy appears and persuades Legree to stop.

Analysis

Chapter 35 portrays the relationship between Cassy and Legree as one fraught with mutual anger and bitterness. Both are aware that Cassy holds a strong and unexplainable influence over Legree, and the slave owner treats her differently from the rest of the slaves. Cassy is intelligent as she is fierce. She challenges Legree's strategy regarding Tom based on a financial logic, which is in the only terms Legree can think.

When Sambo shows Legree the lock of hair, another side of Legree's weakness and superstitions displays itself. Although he fears Cassy, he also is frightened by that part of his past that focuses on his mother. Eva's lock of hair, which resembles his mother's, sends Legree into fits of terror and anguish. Because of her saintly life and death, the image of Legree's mother represents to him an eternal judgment for the worst. He had spurned all that was good in his life.

The description of Legree's sitting room characterizes his own state of mind. The glare from the fireplace shows the "confused and unpromising aspect of the room." The air has a "peculiar sickening, unwholesome smell, compounded of mingled damp, dirt and decay." Cassy's appearance in the room foreshadows Legree's mood of alarm and fear, by which she earlier had made him feel "secretly uneasy, all day."

Legree's terror is heightened by the repetition of seeing a lock of hair. Upon receiving the letter and his mother's hair, he threw them into a fire, as he does again with Eva's locks. Legree even had dreamed of watching his mother's form by his bedside and feeling the lock of hair in his hands.

Chapter 36 also focuses mainly on Cassy and her interaction between the other characters. She first talks to Emmeline and dissuades the younger servant of any intentions to escape. Although an elder, almost motherly figure to Emmeline, Cassy is not quite the mother whom Emmeline is used to. When Legree tried to force Emmeline to drink some of his brandy, she says that her mother had taught her not to indulge in such practices. Cassy regards this comment with disdain, asking Emmeline, "What use is it for mothers to say anything?" Cassy refers to her own history, in which her children had been taken from her. She realizes that as slaves, they have no legal rights to protect their family from harm. Emmeline responds by repeating the phrase that other slaves have made in the book: "I wish I'd never been born!"

Cassy secondly appears to Legree, first in his dream, and then in reality when she attempts to talk him out of beating Tom anymore. When Cassy appears in Legree's dream, the slave holder associates Cassy with the image of his mother. Both women hold a terrifying influence over him that only manages to frighten and enrage him further. After he awakes, Cassy appeals to his greed, thinking that if Tom is crippled, the slave would be incapable of gathering cotton to make a profit for Legree. Cassy realizes the nature of Tom's strength in his religious faith, and she tells Legree that his beatings would do little good anyway. Although Legree sees the sense in her argument, he searches out and strikes Tom until Cassy intervenes.

Cassy thirdly but briefly speaks with Tom, nursing him again after a beating. She warns him that Legree will continue his violence against Tom until the slave either relents or dies. She cares enough for Tom to advise him of what he faces, and even admires his fortitude despite not quite understanding his willingness to die for his faith.

Study Questions

1. Whom does Legree first blame for the misjudgment of beating Tom?

2. What made Legree send Cassy to work in the fields?

3. Why did Cassy return to Legree's house after laboring in the fields?

4. What does Sambo think that Tom's coin and lock of hair are?

5. Of what does Eva's curls remind Legree?

6. What does Emmeline say that she is not afraid of?

7. How does Cassy respond to Emmeline's wishes to escape?

8. How does Emmeline respond to Cassy's longing for death?

9. What does Cassy tell Legree regarding her part in managing the plantation?

10. Why does Cassy know that Tom will never break under Legree's punishment?

Answers

1. Legree first blames Sambo.

2. Cassy argued with Legree over the purchase of Emmeline.

3. She returned to Legree's house to chastise him for beating Tom.

4. He thinks that Tom has a witch's charm.

5. They remind him of his mother's hair, and the moral life from which he had strayed.

6. Emmeline says that she is not afraid of the snakes in the swamps.

7. Cassy responds that the only escape from the plantation is death.

8. Emmeline responds that she considers killing oneself a sin.

9. Cassy tells Legree that she has saved him thousands of dollars by nursing back to health the slaves that he has beaten. She uses this logic to persuade him to stop beating Tom.

10. She knows that Tom will not break under the punishment because of his religious commitment to do right.

Suggested Essay Topics

1. Describe Cassy's influence on Legree. In what ways does she affect him?

2. Discuss Cassy's attitude toward life on the Legree plantation. How do her views affect Emmeline?

3. Analyze Legree's behavior and treatment of Tom in light of Legree's personal history. In what ways does Legree's mother resemble Tom?

Chapter 37

New Characters:

Aunt Dorcas: *Quaker woman who nurses Tom Loker*

Mrs. Smyth: *Quaker woman who helps the Harris family escape to Canada*

Summary

Chapter 37 returns to the Harris family in Ohio. After turning away the slave catchers, they journey to another Quaker settlement and bring the wounded Tom Loker with them. Aunt Dorcas, a "tall, dignified, spiritual woman," nurses Tom Loker, who for three weeks is bedridden from his wounds and a fever. Although he grunts and curses, Aunt Dorcas patiently reminds him to watch his language. To show his appreciation for the Quakers' hospital-

ity, Tom warns them that his slave catching companions are waiting for the Harrises at Sandusky, a northern Ohio town from which
the Harrises plan on departing across Lake Erie to Canada. Jim,
the slave with whom George escaped, goes a different way with
his mother.

George and Eliza Harris take precautions for their escape by
disguising themselves and Harry. Eliza cuts her hair to appear as
a man, while Harry is clothed as a little girl. Mrs. Smyth, a Quaker
woman from Canada, will go with them, posing as Harry's aunt.
Through this ruse, they all hope to evade the slave catchers' attention. George, however, voices his doubts and fears about the
potential failure of the plan. Eliza calms him through her own
religious faith.

The party travels to the docks at Sandusky and remains unde-
tected by Marks, Tom Loker's one-time companion. The Harris family then ride across Lake Erie and safely reach Canada.

Analysis

After the previous chapters' focus on Uncle Tom, this chapter
details Tom Loker's character transformation and the Harris
family's successful escape to Canada. The hospitality of the Quakers affects the health and soul of Tom Loker. Once a harsh and
uncaring slave catcher, he learns from his experience of being left
by Marks and his other companions. A "somewhat sadder and wiser
man," Tom Loker becomes a member in the Quaker settlement,
earning his living as a hunter of animals rather than fugitive slaves.
The Quakers' nursing of Tom Loker reflects their consistency of
doing good for all, a repetition of Simeon Halliday's earlier actions
for the Harris family. The Hallidays would show goodwill to the
slave and slave catcher alike if either were in danger.

When preparing for the final plans of their escape, the Harrises
display a different range of emotions. Eliza is happy that she is with
her husband and child, playfully taking part in making the disguises.
She is also grateful for the Quakers' aid and hospitality. George is
more sulky and worried; he is fearful that the plan might not work.
As a slave, he had known a harsher life than what Eliza had been
used to. For George, the prospect of getting caught and being returned to his brutal master is more than he can fathom, especially

after spending time with his family. Eliza, however, comforts him with her religious faith. George responds: "I will believe you, Eliza...I will believe." From this statement, the reader senses that not only does George have faith in his wife, but may also in God.

The author addresses the theme of liberty for George and for the country as well. Stowe observes that for the people who had fought in the American Revolution, "freedom was the right of a nation to be a nation." For George Harris, liberty means that his family would be protected by law, and that he would be treated as a human being, not as property. An irony appears from the author's viewpoint on slavery. Although Americans had freed themselves from English rule during the American Revolution, they still kept slaves. Those who fled from slavery, like the Harrises, had to escape to Canada. Stowe asks her readers: "What is freedom to a nation, but freedom to the individuals in it?" She suggests that if Americans proclaim themselves as a liberty-loving people, then all, including slaves, must be free.

Study Questions

1. What does Tom Loker grumble about regarding his care by Aunt Dorcas?

2. What does Loker warn Aunt Dorcas about regarding the Harris family?

3. What bothers Aunt Dorcas about Tom Loker's behavior?

4. What concerns does George have about the escape plan?

5. What does Eliza wear to disguise herself as a man?

6. What is Mrs. Smyth's role in the escape plan?

7. From where is Mrs. Smyth originally?

8. What does George overhear as he boards the boat?

9. At which town in Canada does the Harris family arrive?

10. Where do the Harrises stay once they have reached Canada?

Answers

1. He complains that he is too hot because his bed has too many blankets.

2. He warns her that slave catchers are looking out for the Harris family at Sandusky.

3. Loker's cursing bothers her.

4. He is concerned that he and his family will be caught even though they are close to reaching their destination.

5. She wears a cape and some gloves. She also cuts her hair short.

6. She pretends to be the aunt of Harry, who is disguised as a girl.

7. She is originally from a Quaker settlement in Canada.

8. He overhears Marks talking to others to look out for the Harris family.

9. They arrive at Amherstberg.

10. They stay at the home of a missionary.

Suggested Essay Topics

1. Examine the Quakers' influence on Tom Loker. How does their treatment of him compare to how they received the Harrises?

2. Describe the Harris family's reaction once they have landed in Canada.

Chapters 38, 39, and 40

Summary

Chapter 38 centers on Uncle Tom's plight at the Legree plantation. As days and weeks pass, Tom begins to feel his physical and spiritual health declining. He derives little comfort from his Bible, being too weary from heavy labor, and even begins to question whether God had forgotten him.

Simon Legree still torments Tom, telling him: "This yer religion is all a mess of lying trumpery, Tom." Legree's taunts send Tom deeper into despair. Suddenly Tom has a vision of Christ that ap-

pears before him. A voice tells Tom that overcoming earthly sufferings will be rewarded in the heavenly kingdom. From then on, Tom starts to strengthen spiritually and becomes more cheerful. Everyone on the plantation notices this change in Tom's demeanor. Sambo and Legree misinterpret Tom's mood, thinking that he is planning to escape the plantation. Legree becomes angered again and beats Tom, but the slave continues to be at peace with himself. Tom even helps other slaves in the field and preaches to them about his religious faith.

One night, Cassy visits Tom in his cabin. She tells him that Legree has fallen into a drunken sleep. Giving Tom an ax, Cassy states that he could easily murder Legree at this moment. But Tom refuses, saying that killing Legree would be evil and resolve nothing. When Cassy decides to murder Legree herself, Tom dissuades her and advises instead that she should run away.

Chapters 39 and 40 focus on the garret, or attic, of Legree's house and its role in Cassy's escape plans. The garret is a "great, desolate space, dusty, hung with cobwebs, and littered with cast-off lumber." Legree's house servants believe that the place is haunted and are afraid to enter it. A story circulates that one slave woman had once been locked up in the garret for weeks. After she had died and been removed, people continued to hear ghostly moanings and other strange noises.

Cassy decides to use this fear of the garret to her advantage. One day, Cassy moves her furniture out of her bedroom, which is directly beneath the garret. She tells Legree that she cannot sleep because of the banging and groaning upstairs and is moving to another room. Cassy's hints and actions arouse Legree's anxieties. Being very superstitious, Legree struggles with his oncoming fright, sensing that the garret may indeed be haunted.

Cassy stores provisions in the garret, and she tells Emmeline about the escape plans. They will head toward the swamp and lead the search after them, but then circle back to the house and hide in the attic for a while. In the evening, they pretend to run to the swamp. When Legree spots the two fleeing, however, Emmeline almost faints from terror. Cassy pulls a knife on Emmeline, threatening to kill her if she collapses. The two then head for the swamp and double back to the house. Cassy takes some money out of

Legree's desk and the two go up to the garret. Since Legree and the servants are superstitious about the place, Cassy knows that they will not search it or think that the fugitives are hiding up there.

Meanwhile, Legree heads out toward the swamp with a search party, only to return defeated. He repeats the search the next day with the same results. Cassy and Emmeline observe the action from a knothole in the garret wall. After Legree comes back from his second search, he interrogates Tom about the missing women. Tom refuses to tell the whereabouts of his friends, and Legree fatally beats him with the help of Sambo and Quimbo. Later Sambo and Quimbo come to respect and admire Tom's courage. They plead with him to tell them about his religious faith. Although Tom is nearly dead, he manages to convert them, forgiving their past actions against him.

Analysis

In Chapter 38, Tom's faith is sorely tested by Legree's frequent beatings. Tom begins to wonder about his own religious intensity and feels dejected. Legree reminds Tom that the slave could have been one of the managers, but Tom is not comforted by this statement. After this temptation, the vision appears to Tom, offering him the guidance and strength that he needed to continue fighting off Legree's brutality.

Tom's experiences repeat the author's characterization of him as a Christ-like figure. Tom undergoes similar temptations to renounce God and join other faiths. Although tortured and even questioning his own convictions, he ultimately remains steadfast in his beliefs. He is then fortified by the supernatural image and voice of Christ, guaranteeing an everlasting life. Also like Christ, Tom experiences a spiritual bliss that his tormentors misunderstand.

The effect of Tom's spiritual enlightenment also influences the other laborers on the plantation. He helps them through their own sufferings and encourages them with his preaching and hymn singing. At the chapter's end, Tom's encounter with Cassy is the most momentous. Tom rejects her murderous intentions regarding Legree, knowing that if either of them carried out the deed, their souls would be no worse that Legree's. Cassy agrees with Tom, and despite her previous failed attempts at planning an escape, she begins to ponder over one again.

The ingenuity of Cassy is highlighted in Chapters 39 and 40. By playing on the fears of the servants and on Legree himself, she sets the stage for a successful escape. The suspenseful tone of Chapter 39 follows a gothic horror tale, which includes supernatural elements of ghosts and murders, which encourage Legree's anxieties. When Cassy dares Legree to look in the attic, he arms himself with a pistol. The clock strikes forebodingly at midnight, and a wind snuffs out Legree's candle, leaving him in the dark. Cassy even places a book about ghosts on a table where Legree can see it. She also puts an empty bottle in a garret knothole so that when the wind blows, a mournful howl can be heard. All of these incidents fuel Legree's fright.

Cassy's association with Legree is further developed. When Cassy first arrived at Legree's plantation, she was much like Emmeline in character—young and helpless. Cassy's spirit became hardened over time, however, as Legree continued to torment her. But Cassy then reversed the relationship, in which she began to hold a stronger influence over her master. Legree thinks that she is possessed by the devil, an ironic statement coming from a brutish and immoral man such as himself.

Cassy's relationship with Emmeline is deepened by their joint efforts at escape. Cassy displays a toughness that surprises Emmeline. First, when Legree sees them running away, Emmeline feels faint, but Cassy menacingly says that she will kill Emmeline should the girl falter. Cassy knows that if Emmeline does, they will certainly be caught, and either or both of them might wind up dead. Second, after returning to the house, Cassy takes Legree's money for future purchases that they might require. Emmeline's religious upbringing compels her to object to this theft. Cassy rebukes her and argues that both of their lives had been stolen; taking from Legree should be payment for their suffering.

When they reach the safety of the garret, Cassy wonders whether or not her freedom would mean anything to her. After all, she laments that her children had been taken from her, and her own life has been destroyed by slavery. Emmeline lovingly reassures Cassy. Knowing that she probably will never see her own mother again, Emmeline offers herself as Cassy's daughter even if Cassy has lost all hope. Here the theme of rebuilding families after slavery appears and will be repeated later.

In Chapter 40, Tom bears the brunt of Legree's wrath when Cassy and Emmeline cannot be found. Tom again displays his Christ-like qualities, in which he patiently undergoes any torture that Legree, along with Sambo and Quimbo, perform on him. Near the end of life, Tom still manages to forgive and convert Legree's drivers because of his own divine example. This incident recalls Christ's conversion of the two robbers who had been crucified next to him, and emphasizes that anyone can be saved despite their past sinfulness.

Study Questions

1. Why does Legree now work his slaves every day?

2. What is Tom too exhausted to do in his leisure time?

3. What does Legree suggest that Tom do with his Bible?

4. What arouses Tom from his spiritual lethargy?

5. When Tom becomes more cheerful, what explanation does Sambo suggest to Legree for this change?

6. What legend haunts the garret in Legree's house?

7. What does Cassy put into the knothole in the garret?

8. What does Legree notice about the book that Cassy has been reading?

9. Regarding the capture of Cassy and Emmeline, what orders does Legree give to Sambo and Quimbo?

10. Why does Emmeline protest when Cassy steals some money from Legree's desk?

Answers

1. He works the slaves every day because the cotton crop needs harvesting in time to sell on the market.

2. He is too exhausted to read his Bible.

3. Legree suggests that Tom should throw it into the fire.

4. Tom's vision of Christ arouses the slave from his spiritual lethargy.

5. Sambo suggests to Legree that Tom is probably thinking of running away.

6. The legend concerns a slave woman who had incurred Legree's wrath several years ago. He locked her in the garret for weeks, and then the dead woman's body was brought down for burial. Later sounds of violence and despairing groans echoed up in the garret.

7. She puts an empty bottle in the knothole so that when the wind blows, it makes a wailing sound.

8. Legree notices that the book is about murders and ghosts.

9. Legree orders that Cassy may be killed, but not Emmeline.

10. Emmeline protests the stealing of Legree's money because she thinks that it is immoral. Cassy mockingly responds that Legree himself has stolen away slaves' lives.

Suggested Essay Topics

1. Describe Tom's spiritual transformation. Why does he falter in his beliefs? What makes him regain his religious convictions?

2. How does the relationship start and then change between Cassy and Emmeline?

3. Discuss how Cassy plays on Legree's fears and superstitions. Why does Legree react the way he does?

Chapters 41 and 42

New Character:

Madame de Thoux (Emily): *woman whom Master George Shelby meets while heading home, also George Harris's long-lost sister*

Summary

The scene changes to the Shelby plantation, several days after Tom's beating. Mr. Shelby had taken ill and leaves the management

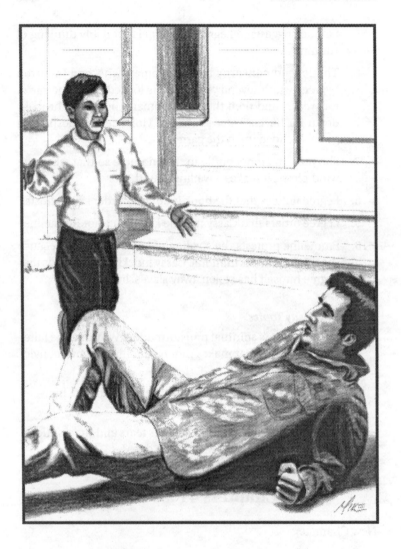

of his estate to his wife. After Mr. Shelby dies, Mrs. Shelby settles the accounts and also receives Miss Ophelia's letter about Uncle Tom. The letter, however, had been delayed for several months, and Tom had already been sold south by the time the Shelbys get the news. Master George, the Shelby's son, travels to New Orleans on some business and decides to also look for Tom. He discovers that Simon Legree had purchased Tom and journeys to the Legree plantation only to find Tom near death. Master George promises to bring Tom back to Kentucky. But knowing it is too late to be reunited with his family, Tom declares a spiritual victory before dying.

Shocked and enraged at Tom's treatment, Master George knocks down Legree and then buries Tom outside the plantation's boundaries. Seeing his devotedness to Tom, other servants of Legree beg Master George to purchase them. Master George cannot, but swears on Tom's grave that he will do his best to end slavery.

After Master George buries Uncle Tom and leaves, the house servants on the Legree plantation begin to hear mysterious whisperings and groanings within the house. Legree is aware of their fears and becomes more frightened himself, locking his bedroom door, drinking heavily, and experiencing more bad dreams. In one nightmare, Legree sees his mother's shroud, or burial sheet, floating before him. But then Cassy appears in the dream, holding that very same shroud. When Legree awakes, a white veiled figure stands in front of him, saying: "Come! come! come!" The figure walks off, and although Legree tests the door, it is still locked. Afterwards, reports gather that Legree is ill and dying from too much drink and hallucinations. Some servants subsequently observe two white veiled figures, who are actually Cassy and Emmeline, heading toward the main road away from the plantation.

Later Cassy and Emmeline, disguised as a Spanish lady and her servant, board a boat sailing north. On the same boat is Master George, who is returning to Kentucky. Cassy and Master George fall into acquaintance, and Cassy eventually confesses to him about her intentions to escape from Legree. Master George, having met the brutal Legree, is sympathetic to the fugitives' plight.

Master George also meets Madame de Thoux, a French woman who is traveling in the same direction. Madame de Thoux discovers that Master George is heading toward Kentucky, and asks him if he knows George Harris. Master George recounts what he can about him and includes the story of Eliza marrying him and running away to Canada. Madame de Thoux shockingly reveals herself as Emily, George Harris's long-lost sister. She had been sold south, but then married her master and moved to the West Indies. Her husband then died, leaving her a fortune.

Cassy overhears some of their conversation, asking Master George about Eliza and from whom she was bought. Master George provides her with some information, and Cassy determines that Eliza is her long-lost daughter.

Analysis

Chapter 41 examines the effects of Tom's death on several characters, especially Master George Shelby. Most of the servants on Legree's plantation are greatly saddened; they try to nurse and comfort Tom in his last moments because he had shown them a better way to live and had given them hope. Sambo and Quimbo are the two who change the most from this episode. Before Tom dies, they realize the savage emptiness of their lives and desire the spiritual nourishment that Tom eventually offers them. The other servants who help Master George with the burial plead with him to purchase them and take them away from Legree.

Legree himself remains somewhat unaffected by Tom's death. When Master George first inquires of Tom, Legree angrily retorts that he had lost money on Tom because of the slave's supposed unruliness and failure to follow Legree's commands. But Legree is also ill at ease in the presence of Master George, knowing that the Kentuckian is a dignified and humane gentleman.

Master George displays the most emotion in this chapter, having known Tom since birth. Along with Mrs. Shelby, he had been against Tom's sale in the first place and had desired to buy back Tom as soon as it was convenient. Arriving too late to help Tom, Master George initially threatens to bring Legree to justice through the courts. But to incriminate Legree, a white person who witnessed Legree's atrocity must testify against him. No such witness exists, however, and Legree mockingly boasts of this shortcoming in Master George's threat. Although plenty of slaves know of Legree's various deeds, they cannot testify in court because of their status as property. Justice is served only when Legree dies from his own torments.

In Chapter 42, Cassy implements her plan to confirm the house inhabitants' belief that the garret is haunted. When the servants hear whispering, the noise is actually from Cassy and Emmeline. Cassy also has the door keys of the house and can, therefore, enter and exit where no one else could go. Her appearance in the sheet only adds to Legree's already disturbed state of mind. The two veiled figures that the servants observe leaving the house are Cassy and Emmeline making their escape, with nobody daring to follow.

The second part of the chapter turns to Cassy and Emmeline in disguise and meeting Master George Shelby on a boat heading north. The author refers to the theme of rebuilding families here. At first, Cassy hides in her cabin so as not to attract too much attention from the other passengers. She only tells Master George of her and Emmeline's situation when he becomes suspicious of their guise. When all of them meet Madame de Thoux, or Emily, the reader begins to see the relationships that each character has toward the others as they reveal their identities. This reunion of family members separated by slavery is coincidental but poignant, since throughout most of the book, families are forced apart.

Study Questions

1. What is Legree's initial reaction to Master George's inquiries about Tom?

2. What had some of Legree's other slaves been doing for Tom?

3. What does Tom request of Master George regarding Tom's family?

4. What does Tom ask of Master George when the boy expresses his anger about Legree?

5. What does Master George bury with Tom?

6. Who are the "ghosts" that haunt the Legree house?

7. What image continues to terrorize Legree?

8. Why does Master George initially offer his assistance to Cassy?

9. What is Madame de Thoux's purpose in going to Kentucky?

10. How does Cassy discover that her daughter Eliza had worked for the Shelbys?

Answers

1. Legree is initially angered by the fact that he lost money on Tom and accuses him of helping Cassy and Emmeline run away.

2. They had been trying their best to nurse Tom, giving him water to drink.

3. Tom requests that Master George not tell Chloe and his family about how he had died since it would cause further grief.

4. Tom asks that Master George not lose his temper at Legree since Tom believes that Legree's soul has already been lost.

5. Master George buries his own cloak with Tom since it is the only thing left that Master George can give him.

6. Cassy and Emmeline are the "ghosts" in Legree's house.

7. The image of his dead mother continues to terrorize him.

8. He initially offers his help to Cassy because he thinks she is ill, although Cassy is pretending so that she can hide in her room and not attract notice.

9. Madame de Thoux's purpose is to search for her brother in Kentucky.

10. Cassy discovers that her daughter had worked for the Shelbys when Master George recounts that Eliza had been bought from a man named Simmons, who sold her away from Cassy.

Suggested Essay Topics

1. Discuss the effects of Legree's brutality and Tom's death on Master George. What does Legree's actions prompt Master George to do regarding slavery?

2. How does Legree's own character contribute to his fears and Cassy's pretense that the house is haunted?

3. Discuss the significance of the discoveries of family-related identities for Madame de Thoux and Cassy.

Chapters 43 and 44

New Character:

Little Eliza: *Eliza and George Harris's daughter*

Summary
Because of their related circumstances, Madame de Thoux and Cassy travel together to Canada to search for their family members. They track the Harris family to Montreal where for the past five years, Eliza and George have lived in freedom. Their son Harry has grown, and the daughter, Little Eliza, is their newest addition to the family. Through the help of a missionary, Madame de Thoux and Cassy are joyfully reunited with the Harrises.

Cassy's character softens once she sees her daughter Eliza and granddaughter Little Eliza. Eliza converts her mother, convincing Cassy of Christianity's moral power. Madame de Thoux offers to share her wealth with the family, and George requests an education. The whole group sails overseas to France, taking Emmeline with them. Emmeline in the meantime meets and falls in love with one of the ship's crew; they ultimately marry. After four years in France, the Harrises return to Canada.

In a letter to a friend, George discusses his plans for the future. He states his sympathy for Africans who have been sold into slavery and determines to go to Africa, claiming that it is where he belongs. He and Eliza, along with the rest of the family, eventually journey there to become missionaries.

The reader also learns that Miss Ophelia took Topsy back to Vermont and freed her. Topsy received an education and was baptized; she then travels to Africa, like the Harrises, to become a missionary.

Meanwhile, Master George returns to Kentucky and tells the sad news about Tom to Mrs. Shelby and Aunt Chloe. Some months later, Master George gathers the servants together and tells them that he has drawn up papers to free them all. The ones who stay at the plantation receive wages for their labor, never having to worry any longer about the uncertainties of slavery if anything happens to Master George. Reminding them of Uncle Tom's goodness, Master George tells his workers that he had promised on Tom's grave that he would never own any more slaves, and that they should be thankful to Tom.

Analysis

Chapters 43 and 44 summarize the converging stories of the book. After the horrific trials of abuse, uncertainty, and escape, the Harris family reunites in Canada to live fuller lives. The theme of Christianity and the family is important here. Even before Madame de Thoux and Cassy arrive, George and Eliza are contented with their life in freedom. Cassy is welcomed into the Christian fold through her family despite her earlier doubts about religion. With the entrance of the long-lost relatives, the Harrises decide to move to Africa and become missionaries. Topsy, like Cassy, had rejected any religious doctrines because of her harsh existence under slavery. But like the Harrises, she also travels to Africa to be a missionary.

George's letter to an unnamed friend outlines his philosophy on the theme of freedom and slavery. He is aware that as a fugitive, he cannot return to America and that his efforts to fight against slavery there would be useless. By journeying to Africa, George rejects his white lineage and sets out to found a Christian nation there. The theme of religion is important to George's mission. As he writes: "I trust that the development of Africa is to be essentially a Christian one."

Uncle Tom's life and death affect Master George to the extent that the young man frees the Shelbys' slaves. Master George learns from Tom's experiences that even with kind masters, slaves are better off with their own freedom. He also knows that because of his father's financial debts and St. Clare's untimely death, Tom ultimately endured untold hardships and finally death because of their indirect carelessness and Simon Legree's harshness. Master George determines not to make the same mistakes, and by emancipating his servants, begins his stand against slavery.

Study Questions

1. What occupation does George have in Canada?

2. Who are the Harrises' visitors when they are sitting down for tea?

3. How does Cassy react when she sees her granddaughter Little Eliza?

4. What does George desire when his sister Emily provides him with funds?

5. Although George is a mulatto, his father being white and his mother black, where do his sympathies lie?

6. Why does George opt to help Africans rather that enslaved blacks in America?

7. What makes Mrs. Shelby uneasy when she receives a letter from Master George, who is on his way home?

8. What does Aunt Chloe do with the money she had raised to buy Tom when she finally hears of his death?

9. What does Master George eventually do for his servants?

10. Why does Master George attribute the servants' freedom to Tom?

Answers

1. He is a machinist.

2. Madame de Thoux and Cassy, along with a missionary, are the Harrises' visitors.

3. Cassy takes Little Eliza in her arms, saying "Darling, I'm your mother!" She blurts this out because to Cassy, Little Eliza looks like Eliza did when Cassy had last seen her daughter.

4. He desires an education.

5. George states that his sympathies lie with the blacks since they are oppressed.

6. He opts to help Africans because he feels that as an individual he cannot do much in America. But he hopes to gain

anti-slavery supporters in Africa and call attention to the plight of slaves in America.

7. Mrs. Shelby becomes uneasy when her son has little to say about Tom in his letter. She comes to believe that something terrible has happened.

8. Chloe says that she never wants to see or hear of the money again.

9. He eventually frees them all so that they will not have to face the uncertainties and horrors of slavery.

10. He attributes the servants' freedom to Tom because of the self-sacrificing example of his death.

Suggested Essay Topics

1. Describe the changes that members of the Harris family endure. How have George and Eliza changed? How has Cassy?

2. Examine Master George's actions for his servants. What experiences of Tom's makes Master George hate slavery?

Chapter 45

Summary

In this final chapter, Harriet Beecher Stowe provides incidents and observations that led her to the writing of Uncle Tom's Cabin. The characters of Eliza Harris and Uncle Tom, she notes, were drawn from her own personal knowledge. One of Stowe's brothers supplied the anecdotes on which she based Old Prue and Simon Legree. A slave mother's crossing of the ice-packed Ohio River had also been taken from a real-life occurrence. Stowe points out that Uncle Tom's experience of being legally unprotected was a common one among slaves. The sale of mulatto women as slave mistresses was also a well-known practice among Southerners.

The greatest factor that led the author to write her book was the passage of the Fugitive Slave Law in 1850. Appealing to her

Northern and Southern readers, Stowe emphasizes the inconsistency of practicing Christianity, with its call for the moral and humane treatment of all, while simultaneously hunting down runaway slaves. She challenges Southerners to think through their moral conscience and implores Northerners to welcome escaped slaves and educate them. The author claims that by participating in the Fugitive Slave Law, both sides have sinned in the eyes of God and must atone by fighting against the system of slavery.

Analysis

At the time of Uncle Tom's Cabin's publication, some Northern and Southern readers felt uneasy about the author's rendition of slavery in the Old South. Many Southerners were defensive about anyone attacking the forced labor system, stating that slaves were not mistreated. They based their arguments on the laws of property: no one would abuse their property because it would be financially ruinous to the owners themselves. The fact that Stowe presented evidence against this line of reasoning, writing that no legal protection exists for slaves, made Southern readers all the more angry.

Some Northerners were also unhappy with Stowe's portrait of their region's participation in slavery. Throughout the novel, the author accuses Northerners of actively engaging slavery through legal compromises such as the Fugitive Slave Law. Stowe also indicts the system that supported slavery, from legislatures that pass the laws to hypocrites willing to attack slavery, but not do anything to help the slaves.

By summarizing some of her historical sources, the author hoped to prove the general validity of her claim about the evils of slavery. Stowe pleads directly with the reader to live by the ideals presented in the theme of law and religion, combining legal rights with Christian morals. She uses polemical, or argumentative, language to make strong points against slavery and force her readers to think as religious people about the plight of slaves. The writer assertively asks: "What do you owe to these poor unfortunates, oh Christians?"

Study Questions

1. Why does the author include real life incidents in the final chapter?

2. With what anecdote did the author's brother provide her regarding the character for Simon Legree?

3. What does Stowe say is the only thing that would protect a slave from abuse?

4. What law prompted Stowe to write Uncle Tom's Cabin?

5. What effects does slavery have on its victims?

6. What is the most sought after goal that freed slaves desire?

7. Where did Stowe gain some of her personal knowledge of slavery?

8. How does the author view the role of the church?

9. What is the author's intent by listing several free blacks' occupations?

10. Where does the author think is a good refuge for freed and escaped slaves?

Answers

1. She includes these incidents because some of her readers have inquired whether her story had been based on facts.

2. Stowe's brother recounted an incident in which a slave holder displayed his own fist with which he used to knock down slaves.

3. She states that only a master's character can protect a slave from abuse.

4. The Fugitive Slave Law prompts Stowe to write her book.

5. She cites that slavery destroys the hearts and minds of the slaves, as well as breaking up families.

6. They desire education.

7. She gains her knowledge of slavery from living in Ohio, on "the frontier-line of slave states."

8. She viewed the church as the provider of intellectual and moral education.

9. Her intent was to show that freed slaves were capable of working on their own and earning a living.

10. She thinks that Africa is a good refuge.

Suggested Essay Topics

1. Compare and contrast Stowe's views on the North and South. What aspects of each does she criticize?

2. How do her personal life and knowledge affect the author's portrayal of slavery?

Sample Analytical Paper Topics

Topic #1

In Uncle Tom's Cabin, Harriet Beecher Stowe emphasizes that the effects of slavery are as tragic for the slave as for the slave holder. Discuss why Mr. Shelby and Augustine St. Clare are ambivalent figures because of their involvement in slavery.

Outline

I. Thesis Statement: *Mr. Shelby and Augustine St. Clare are ambivalent figures because despite being humane slave owners, they unwittingly contribute to their slaves' miseries.*

II. The slave owners' humanity

    A. Both treat their slaves humanely

    B. Mr. Shelby repulsed by Haley the slave trader

    C. St. Clare knows slavery is wrong

    D. St. Clare exposes Miss Ophelia's hypocritical stance on slavery

III. The slave owners' carelessness

    A. Mr. Shelby falls into debt and must sell Tom and Harry

    B. Mr. Shelby refuses help from his wife

    C. St. Clare opposes slavery, but cannot free his slaves

    D. St. Clare stalls at writing Tom's free papers and dies

IV. Their unintentional effects on Uncle Tom

    A. Mr. Shelby separates Tom from his family

    B. St. Clare dies and Simon Legree buys Tom

Topic #2

    Uncle Tom and Eva St. Clare can be considered as saintly martyrs. Explain how each fits this description with regard to slavery and religion, referring to examples from the book.

Outline

I.   Thesis Statement: *Uncle Tom and Eva St. Clare are saintly martyrs because both share the qualities of Christ-like piety: sacrificing their lives to help others, being generous, humble, and forgiving.*

II.   Uncle Tom

    A. Understanding and forgiving of Mr. Shelby for selling him

    B. Calms anger of Aunt Chloe and Master George

    C. Helps other laborers on the Legree plantation

    D. Stops Cassy from killing Legree

    E. Pities Legree while suffering beatings and death

III. Little Eva

    A. Wants to buy Tom to make him happy

    B. Befriends and loves Topsy when no one else does

    C. Convinces Henrique St. Clare to love Dodo

    D. Indirectly influences Miss Ophelia to love Topsy

    E. Tries to convert her father, Augustine St. Clare

    F. On her deathbed, tells servants to live and love as Christians

Topic #3

Throughout the book, the author emphasizes the importance of family to argue against the evils of slavery. By providing examples of families in the novel, show how Harriet Beecher Stowe connects this theme of family to counter slavery.

Outline

I. Thesis Statement: *Harriet Beecher Stowe argues against slavery by depicting slaves as having families. The author thus personalizes the problem and gains the readers' sympathy through their own familial experiences.*

II. Uncle Tom's family

  A. Tom as a family man

  B. Portrayal of Aunt Chloe and their children

III. The Harris family

  A. Eliza runs away with Harry to protect her only son

  B. George Harris runs away

    1. promises to buy his wife and child

IV. The Shelby family

  A. Mrs. Shelby

    1. teaches religion to slaves

    2. raises Eliza almost like a daughter

    3. opposes breaking families through sales of Tom and Harry

V. The Bird family

  A. Mrs. Bird

    1. argues religious morality with husband, Senator Bird

    2. thinks of own departed son when helping Eliza

SECTION FOUR

Bibliography

Hedrick, Joan D. Harriet Beecher Stowe: *A Life*. New York: Oxford University Press, 1994.

Stowe, Harriet Beecher. *Uncle Tom's Cabin*. Boston and Cleveland: John P. Jewett & Co., 1852; reprint ed., New York: Harper & Row, 1965.

Sundquist, Eric J., ed. *New Essays on Uncle Tom's Cabin*. Cambridge, Eng.: Cambridge University Press, 1986.

MAXnotes®

REA's Literature Study Guides

MAXnotes® are student-friendly. They offer a fresh look at masterpieces of literature, presented in a lively and interesting fashion. **MAXnotes®** offer the essentials of what you should know about the work, including outlines, explanations and discussions of the plot, character lists, analyses, and historical context. **MAXnotes®** are designed to help you think independently about literary works by raising various issues and thought-provoking ideas and questions. Written by literary experts who currently teach the subject, **MAXnotes®** enhance your understanding and enjoyment of the work.

Available **MAXnotes®** include the following:

Absalom, Absalom!	Heart of Darkness	Of Mice and Men
The Aeneid of Virgil	Henry IV, Part I	On the Road
Animal Farm	Henry V	Othello
Antony and Cleopatra	The House on Mango Street	Paradise Lost
As I Lay Dying	Huckleberry Finn	A Passage to India
As You Like It	I Know Why the Caged	Plato's Republic
The Autobiography of	Bird Sings	Portrait of a Lady
Malcolm X	The Iliad	A Portrait of the Artist
The Awakening	Invisible Man	as a Young Man
Beloved	Jane Eyre	Pride and Prejudice
Beowulf	Jazz	A Raisin in the Sun
Billy Budd	The Joy Luck Club	Richard II
The Bluest Eye, A Novel	Jude the Obscure	Romeo and Juliet
Brave New World	Julius Caesar	The Scarlet Letter
The Canterbury Tales	King Lear	Sir Gawain and the
The Catcher in the Rye	Les Misérables	Green Knight
The Color Purple	Lord of the Flies	Slaughterhouse-Five
The Crucible	Macbeth	Song of Solomon
Death in Venice	The Merchant of Venice	The Sound and the Fury
Death of a Salesman	The Metamorphoses of Ovid	The Stranger
The Divine Comedy I: Inferno	The Metamorphosis	The Sun Also Rises
Dubliners	Middlemarch	A Tale of Two Cities
Emma	A Midsummer Night's Dream	Taming of the Shrew
Euripedes' Electra & Medea	Moby-Dick	The Tempest
Frankenstein	Moll Flanders	Tess of the D'Urbervilles
Gone with the Wind	Mrs. Dalloway	Their Eyes Were Watching God
The Grapes of Wrath	Much Ado About Nothing	To Kill a Mockingbird
Great Expectations	My Antonia	To the Lighthouse
The Great Gatsby	Native Son	Twelfth Night
Gulliver's Travels	1984	Uncle Tom's Cabin
Hamlet	The Odyssey	Waiting for Godot
Hard Times	Oedipus Trilogy	Wuthering Heights

RESEARCH & EDUCATION ASSOCIATION
61 Ethel Road W. • Piscataway, New Jersey 08854
Phone: (908) 819-8880

Please send me more information about MAXnotes®.

Name _____

Address _____

City _____ State _____ Zip _____